The Big Book of Tarot

Victor Denis Purcell

Published by Victor Denis Purcell, 2024.

While every precaution has been taken in the preparation of this book, the publisher assumes no responsibility for errors or omissions, or for damages resulting from the use of the information contained herein.

THE BIG BOOK OF TAROT

First edition. June 11, 2024.

Copyright © 2024 Victor Denis Purcell.

ISBN: 979-8227607591

Written by Victor Denis Purcell.

Dedicated to: Matt, Taylor and Alexander

The Big Book of Tarot
By Victor Denis Purcell

Synopsis

This comprehensive guide to tarot is a treasure trove of wisdom and insight, perfect for beginners and seasoned practitioners. It delves into the multifaceted world of tarot, covering every aspect, from its rich symbolism to practical reading techniques.

The book begins by exploring the intricate tapestry of symbolism inherent in tarot cards. It breaks down common themes, colors, numbers, and imagery, illuminating how these elements blend to create profound meanings in each reading. This section offers a deep understanding of the language of tarot, providing readers with the tools to interpret the cards more intuitively.

The guide then navigates through various tarot decks, such as the iconic Rider-Waite, the mystical Thoth, and the traditional Marseille. It highlights how each deck's unique imagery and symbolism bring different dimensions to readings, helping readers choose a deck that resonates most with their style and needs.

Readers are introduced to various tarot spreads, from the classic Celtic Cross to the concise Three-Card Spread. This section not only explains how to lay out cards but also delves into the art of framing questions and interpreting card combinations, enriching the tarot reading experience.

The book explores the fascinating interplay between tarot and astrology, revealing how tarot cards correlate with astrological signs and planets. This section broadens the reader's perspective, offering a holistic approach to understanding the cards in the context of the more expansive universe.

Drawing on Jungian psychology and other psychological theories, this part delves into the use of tarot for self-reflection, therapy, and personal growth. It examines how tarot can be a powerful tool for introspection and mental well-being, making it relevant not just for spiritual exploration but also for psychological self-care.

Practicality meets spirituality in this section, which offers advice on creating the ideal environment for tarot readings. It covers everything from arranging physical spaces to grounding techniques, ensuring that readers can practice tarot in settings that are both conducive and ethically sound.

This crucial chapter addresses the ethical responsibilities of tarot readers. It emphasizes the importance of dealing with sensitive topics with care, maintaining client confidentiality, and adhering to a code of ethics, ensuring that readings are conducted with integrity and respect.

The guide takes a serene turn, exploring how tarot can be incorporated into meditation and mindfulness practices. It suggests using the imagery of tarot cards for visualization and contemplation, offering a unique approach to meditation and tarot reading.

This chapter is a goldmine for beginners and those curious about tarot, addressing common questions and clearing up misconceptions. It provides clear, concise answers that are both informative and reassuring, making the world of tarot more accessible.

Concluding the book is a comprehensive list of resources for further learning. From recommended books and websites to courses and communities, this section guides readers toward deepening their tarot knowledge and practice, providing pathways for continued exploration and growth.

In summary, this book is a meticulous and insightful guide that covers every angle of the tarot world. It promises to be an invaluable resource for anyone looking to deepen their understanding of tarot, whether taking their first steps into this mystical art or seeking to enrich their established practice.

Chapter headings

Introduction

Welcome to the enchanting world of tarot, where symbolism, intuition, and insight intertwine to reveal the deeper truths of our lives and choices. This book is your guide through this mystical journey. It comprehensively explores tarot's many facets, from its rich symbolism and diverse decks to practical reading techniques and ethical considerations.

Tarot, an ancient practice steeped in mystery and wisdom, has captivated knowledge seekers for centuries. Its allure lies in how it mirrors our lives, relationships, and innermost thoughts. Through the pages of this book, you will embark on a journey to unlock the secrets of the tarot, a journey that promises to be as transformative as it is enlightening.

As we delve into the symbolism of tarot, you will discover a language that speaks through vibrant imagery, archetypal themes, and a spectrum of colors and numbers. This language is not just about predicting the future; it's a tool for understanding your present, reflecting on your past, and contemplating the possibilities.

The world of tarot decks is as varied as it is fascinating. From the traditional Rider-Waite and the mystical Thoth to the classic Marseille, each deck brings its unique flavor and perspective to readings. This book guides you through these differences, helping you find the deck that resonates most profoundly with your spirit and style.

Understanding tarot spreads and reading techniques is crucial for beginners and experienced readers. This guide breaks down various spreads, explaining how each layout is suited for different types of questions and readings. You'll learn how to frame questions effectively and interpret card combinations in a way that brings clarity and depth to your readings.

Chapter 1: Tarot and Symbolism

Explore the rich symbolism in tarot, including common themes, colors, numbers, and imagery, and how they contribute to interpreting the cards.

Tarot is more than a divinatory tool; it's a pathway to personal growth and self-reflection. Drawing on psychological theories, particularly Jungian psychology, this book explores how tarot can be used as a powerful tool for self-exploration, therapy, and personal development, helping you to navigate the complexities of your psyche and life's journey.

Practical tips for conducting tarot readings are essential for creating an authentic and meaningful experience. This guide advises setting the right environment for your readings, grounding techniques, and ethical considerations, ensuring your tarot practice is respectful and impactful.

Ethics and responsibility are the cornerstones of tarot reading. This book addresses the importance of compassionately dealing with sensitive topics, maintaining client confidentiality, and adhering to a code of ethics. These principles help in nurturing a practice that is not only insightful but also respectful and empowering for those seeking guidance.

Tarot can be a contemplative tool, aiding in mindfulness practices. This book explores using tarot imagery for visualization and meditation, providing a unique approach to achieving mental clarity and emotional balance.

Tarot cards are a fascinating and intricate tool for divination, reflection, and psychological exploration, steeped in rich symbolism and multilayered meanings. Each card in a tarot deck is a tapestry of symbols, colors, numbers, and imagery, each contributing to its overall interpretation. Let's delve into these aspects to understand better how they contribute to the art of tarot reading.

The Major and Minor Arcana: The tarot deck is divided into two main sections - the Major Arcana and the Minor Arcana. The Major Arcana consists of 22 cards, each representing significant life themes and lessons. These cards often feature archetypal figures and scenarios that embody universal human experiences. The Minor Arcana, comprising 56 cards, reflects day-to-day events and is further divided into four suits (Cups, Wands, Swords, and Pentacles), each associated with an element (Water, Fire, Air, and Earth, respectively).

Symbolism of Colors: Color symbolism is pivotal in tarot. For instance, red often represents passion, energy, and action, while blue symbolizes calmness, spirituality, and introspection. Green, commonly seen in the suit of Pentacles, signifies growth, nature, and material well-being. Using color in tarot is not arbitrary; it deliberately conveys deeper meanings and emotional undertones.

Numerology in Tarot: Numbers on tarot cards are deeply symbolic. Each number has its significance – ones (or Aces) generally symbolize new beginnings, twos indicate balance or duality, threes are associated with growth and expansion, and so on. In a reading, the number on a card can offer insight into the stage of a situation or the intensity of the energy surrounding it.

Imagery and Symbols: The imagery on tarot cards is rich and varied, incorporating a range of symbols from various cultures and esoteric traditions. Common symbols include animals (like lions for courage or rabbits for fertility), natural elements (such as water for emotions or mountains for challenges), and objects (like swords for conflict or cups for emotions). These images aren't just decorative; they're keys to understanding the more profound message of the card.

The Role of Archetypes: Many tarot cards incorporate archetypal figures and scenarios, drawing from mythology, religion, and psychology. These archetypes – such as The Empress, symbolizing fertility and nurturing, or The Hermit, representing introspection and wisdom – tap into our collective unconscious and provide a universal language for understanding our experiences and the world around us.

The Four Elements and Suits: Each suit in the Minor Arcana is associated with an element – Cups with Water, Wands with Fire, Swords with Air, and Pentacles with Earth. This elemental association adds another layer of meaning to the cards. For example, Cups deal with emotional matters (reflecting the fluidity of water), while Swords concern intellect and conflict (echoing the cutting and ethereal nature of air).

Court Cards and Personalities: The Court Cards (Kings, Queens, Knights, and Pages) in each suit reflect different personality types or aspects of the self. The King of Wands, for example, might represent a charismatic leader, while the Queen of Swords could symbolize a perceptive, sharp-witted individual. These cards can represent people in the querent's life or aspects of their personality.

The Journey of the Fool: The Fool's journey through the Major Arcana is a metaphor for the human experience, representing our journey from innocence and ignorance (The Fool) to enlightenment and understanding (The World). Each card in the Major Arcana represents a stage or lesson in this journey, reflecting the challenges, joys, and transformations we encounter.

Historical and Cultural Influences: The symbolism in tarot cards is not just mystical but also historical and cultural. Many decks draw on various traditions, from medieval European iconography to Eastern mysticism, reflecting the diverse influences shaping the tarot's development over centuries.

Personal and Intuitive Interpretation: While traditional meanings and symbols are essential, tarot reading is also deeply personal and intuitive. Readers might interpret a card slightly differently based on their experiences and insights. This personal connection to the cards makes tarot a uniquely powerful tool for self-reflection and understanding.

These layers of symbolism, from the macrocosm of the Major and Minor Arcana to the microcosm of colors, numbers, and images, make the tarot a complex and rich tool for divination and self-discovery. Whether you are a seasoned reader or a curious beginner, the tarot offers a window into the subconscious, helping to illuminate the hidden corners of our minds and the mysteries of our lives.

Historical perspective, journey, through the centuries.

The history and evolution of tarot cards is a complex and intriguing subject that intertwines with various cultural and historical narratives. Tracing their journey from early beginnings to their role in modern society reveals how these cards have transcended their initial purposes to become a multifaceted tool of symbolism, self-reflection, and divination.

Chapter 2: Different Tarot Decks and Their Significance

Discuss various tarot decks available, such as the Rider-Waite, Thoth, and Marseille, and how their imagery and symbolism differ.

The precise origins of tarot cards remain shrouded in mystery and speculation. It is widely believed that they emerged in Northern Italy during the 15th century, originally conceived as a card game called Tarocchi. These first tarot decks were luxuriously hand-painted, a testament to the craftsmanship of the era and a treasure for the wealthy patrons who commissioned them. The imagery depicted on these cards was deeply rooted in the medieval worldview, infused with symbolic and religious symbolism reflective of that time. Over time, these cards spread across Europe, gaining popularity in countries like France and Spain.

As tarot cards gained prominence, their usage gradually shifted from mere entertainment to a more mystical and esoteric domain. By the late 18th century, there was a growing belief, mainly propelled by figures such as Antoine Court de Gébelin, that tarot cards held more profound, more ancient wisdom. Gébelin's theories, although lacking concrete historical evidence, suggested that the tarot had connections to the mysteries of ancient Egypt, thus imbuing the cards with an aura of mystical knowledge. This era marked a significant turning point, as the cards began to be viewed not just as a pastime but as a tool for divination and accessing hidden truths.

In the 19th and early 20th centuries, we witnessed a resurgence in interest in the occult and mystical arts in Europe, especially within circles in France and England. This period saw the creation and popularization of several esoteric tarot decks, the most notable being the Rider-Waite-Smith deck. Crafted by A.E. Waite and artistically rendered by Pamela Colman Smith, this deck stood out due to its detailed illustrations, especially in the Minor Arcana, which had not been given much attention in earlier decks. The Rider-Waite-Smith deck, with its rich symbolism and accessible imagery, revolutionized tarot reading and solidified its role in the practice of divination.

There are certain pioneers in this field, which include

Rider-Waite Tarot Deck:

The Rider-Waite Tarot deck, also known as the Rider Tarot or Waite-Smith Tarot, was created by Arthur Edward Waite, a British occultist, and Pamela Colman Smith, an artist, in the early 20th century. Waite, a prominent member of the Hermetic Order of the Golden Dawn, sought to create a tarot deck accessible to a broader audience. He provided the guidebook, "The Pictorial Key to the Tarot," which explained the symbolism and interpretations of the cards straightforwardly. Smith, a talented artist, illustrated the deck with vibrant and evocative imagery that brought the archetypal symbolism to life. The Rider-Waite Tarot deck quickly gained popularity and became a standard reference for tarot readings due to its intuitive symbolism and comprehensive guidebook.

Marseille Tarot Deck:

The Marseille Tarot deck is one of the oldest and most influential tarot decks, originating in the 17th century in France. While the individuals responsible for its creation are unknown, the Marseille Tarot deck represents a traditional style characterized by its simple yet powerful imagery. The deck consists of symbolic illustrations on the cards, emphasizing the use of intuition and personal interpretation during readings. The Marseille Tarot deck has significantly impacted the development and evolution of tarot throughout history, serving as a foundation for many subsequent tarot decks. Its timeless and archetypal symbolism continues to resonate with readers, offering a direct and profound connection to the wisdom of the tarot tradition.

Each deck has its unique style, symbolism, and interpretation, making it popular among tarot enthusiasts and practitioners. Exploring the differences between these decks allows readers to choose the one that resonates with them and aligns with their preferred approach to tarot readings. Whether one is drawn to the intuitive and accessible imagery of the Rider-Waite Tarot, the mystical and esoteric insights of the Thoth Tarot, or the traditional and archetypal symbolism of the Marseille Tarot, each deck offers a rich and transformative journey into the world of tarot.

These styles are presented below in more detail:

Rider-Waite Tarot Deck:

The Rider-Waite Tarot deck, also known as the Rider Tarot or Waite-Smith Tarot, was created by Arthur Edward Waite, a British occultist, and Pamela Colman Smith, an artist, in the early 20th century. Waite, a prominent member of the Hermetic Order of the Golden Dawn, sought to create a tarot deck accessible to a broader audience. He provided the guidebook, "The Pictorial Key to the Tarot," which explained the symbolism and interpretations of the cards straightforwardly. Smith, a talented artist, illustrated the deck with vibrant and evocative imagery that brought the archetypal symbolism to life. The Rider-Waite Tarot deck quickly gained popularity and became a standard reference for tarot readings due to its intuitive symbolism and comprehensive guidebook.

Marseille Tarot Deck:

The Marseille Tarot deck is one of the oldest and most influential tarot decks, originating in the 17th century in France. While the individuals responsible for its creation are unknown, the Marseille Tarot deck represents a traditional style characterized by its simple yet powerful imagery. The deck consists of symbolic illustrations on the cards, emphasizing the use of intuition and personal interpretation during readings. The Marseille Tarot deck has significantly impacted the development and evolution of tarot throughout history, serving as a foundation for many subsequent tarot decks. Its timeless and archetypal symbolism continues to resonate with readers, offering a direct and profound connection to the wisdom of the tarot tradition.

Each deck has its unique style, symbolism, and interpretation, making it popular among tarot enthusiasts and practitioners. Exploring the differences between these decks allows readers to choose the one that resonates with them and aligns with their preferred approach to tarot readings. Whether one is drawn to the intuitive and accessible imagery of the Rider-Waite Tarot, the mystical and esoteric insights of the Thoth Tarot, or the traditional and archetypal symbolism of the Marseille Tarot, each deck offers a rich and transformative journey into the world of tarot.

There are many more styles of card spreads. I will present nine of them below:

One Card Spread

The One Card Spread is the essence of simplicity, making it ideal for quick insights and daily guidance. In this spread, the single card drawn can offer a clear and focused answer to a specific question or a thought for the day. The interpretation hinges on the symbolism and meaning of the card drawn. For example, illustrating The Sun might suggest a day filled with positivity and vitality, while The Tower could indicate a day of unexpected changes. This spread benefits beginners or those seeking clarity without the complexity of multiple cards.

Horseshoe Spread

The Horseshoe Spread provides a more comprehensive view,

typically used for more complex questions. The seven cards cover different aspects: past influences, the present situation, future potential, obstacles, external influences, hopes/fears, and potential outcomes. For instance, if the 'past' card is The Fool, it might suggest a period of naivety or new beginnings, influencing the current situation. The 'obstacle' card can pinpoint challenges to be aware of. The final card, indicating potential outcomes, ties together the narrative suggested by the preceding cards, offering a rounded perspective on the query.

Star Spread

The Star Spread, with its six-card star-shaped layout, is ideal for deep dives into specific issues or questions. Each card represents a facet of the problem or question, providing a layered understanding. The cards might represent current influences, hopes, hidden factors, immediate next steps, external influences, and potential outcomes. The interpretation involves understanding how these facets interact. For example, a card like The Hermit in the 'hidden factors' position might suggest introspection, while The Chariot in the 'next steps' position could indicate that assertive action is needed.

Concurrent with the rise of esoteric tarot was an effort to integrate the cards with other astrology. This synthesis was part of a more significant movement to create a comprehensive mystical framework, with the tarot as a critical component. Groups like the Hermetic Order of the Golden Dawn were instrumental in this endeavor, incorporating the tarot into their mystical practices. The integration of these systems imbued the tarot with even deeper layers of meaning and expanded its use beyond mere fortune-telling to a tool for spiritual and personal development.

In the 20th century, tarot cards continued to evolve, mirroring the broader shifts in society and culture. New decks began to move away from traditional Christian and medieval symbolism, embracing more contemporary and diverse imagery. This period, they have also marked the recognition of tarot as a valuable tool for psychoanalysis and self-reflection. Influenced by the psychological theories of Carl Jung, who recognized the power of symbolism and archetypes, tarot reading began to be seen as a way to explore the subconscious mind and facilitate personal growth.

Recent years have seen a significant movement towards creating inclusive tarot decks representing various cultures, genders, and perspectives. This trend reflects a broader societal shift towards embracing diversity and ensuring representation in multiple forms of media and expression. Contemporary tarot decks often draw on diverse mythologies, cultures, and artistic movements, offering a more global and inclusive perspective. This evolution of tarot imagery not only broadens its appeal but also enriches the depth and relevance of its symbolism.

The digital age has ushered in a new era for tarot cards. Online tarot readings and digital versions of tarot decks have become increasingly popular, making the practice more accessible worldwide. This digitalization of tarot has opened up new avenues for exploration and interpretation, allowing for a fusion of traditional practices with modern technology. It has also facilitated the creation of online communities where enthusiasts can share insights, interpretations, and experiences, further expanding the reach and influence of tarot.

Today, tarot cards are not just seen as a mystical tool but have also permeated various aspects of popular culture. They appear in art, literature, movies, and even fashion, reflecting the enduring fascination with their symbolism and the human desire for understanding and introspection. The journey of tarot from Renaissance Italy to today's digital screens showcases its remarkable adaptability and enduring appeal. As a tool for divination, self-exploration, and artistic expression, tarot cards continue to captivate and inspire, holding a unique place in historical and contemporary contexts.

Chapter 3: The Connection Between Tarot and Astrology

Delve into how tarot is related to astrology, including how the cards correspond to different astrological signs and planets.

Exploring the parallels between astrology and tarot reveals a deep well of shared symbolism and thematic overlaps. These two ancient practices, both rich in symbolism and steeped in archetypal imagery, offer unique yet interconnected paths to understanding human experiences and personalities.

Astrology and tarot are deeply rooted in the concept of archetypes, serving as mirrors of human experiences and personality traits. In astrology, these archetypes manifest as planets and zodiac signs, with each celestial body and sign symbolizing different aspects of human life and character. For example, Venus represents love and beauty, while Scorpio may signify mystery and transformation. Similarly, the Major Arcana in Tarot is a collection of archetypal images and themes. Cards like The Empress embody nurturing and abundance, akin to the fertile qualities of Earth signs in astrology. This shared language of archetypes allows both astrology and tarot to speak to the universal aspects of the human condition, offering insights into our inner workings and external circumstances.

The four classical elements of Earth, Water, Air, and Fire are integral to astrology and tarot, providing a framework for understanding different energies and characteristics. In astrology, each zodiac sign is associated with one of these elements, shaping its traits and behaviors. Earth signs, for instance, are known for their grounded and pragmatic approach to life, while Air signs are often intellectual and communicative. In the realm of tarot, the Minor Arcana is divided into four suits, each corresponding to these elements: Pentacles (Earth), Cups (Water), Swords (Air), and Wands (Fire). The elemental qualities influence the cards' meanings, with Earthy Pentacles often relating to material aspects of life and Fiery Wands to creativity and action. This elementary framework provides a common ground for interpreting and understanding the various aspects of both practices.

Many tarot cards are closely linked to specific planetary energies in astrology, enriching their meanings and interpretations. The Moon card, for instance, shares a connection with the astrological moon, echoing themes of intuition, the subconscious, and the emotional realm. Similarly, The Tower card can be associated with the transformative power of Pluto, representing sudden change and upheaval. These planetary correspondences in tarot offer a deeper dimension to card readings, allowing for a more nuanced understanding that parallels astrological interpretations.

In certain tarot decks, the Major Arcana cards are explicitly connected to the zodiac signs, adding an astrological layer to their interpretation. This linkage enables a synthesis of tarot symbolism with astrological insights. The Strength card, often linked to Leo, emphasizes themes of courage and vitality, mirroring the bold and expressive traits of the Leo sign. By understanding these astrological associations, one can gain a more comprehensive perspective on the cards, seeing them not just as isolated symbols but as part of a broader cosmic narrative.

Astrology and tarot serve not only as tools for prediction but also as mediums for reflection and personal growth. They offer a lens through which individuals can explore potential future paths, but more importantly, they provide a space for introspection and self-discovery. This reflective aspect is central to both practices, encouraging users to look inward and contemplate their journeys and challenges. In astrology, a natal chart can reveal inherent strengths and weaknesses, life lessons, and the soul's purpose. At the same time, a tarot spread can offer guidance, clarity, and perspective on one's current life situation and potential future developments.

Both astrology and tarot emphasize the importance of cycles, transitions, and the dynamic nature of life. In astrology, these cycles are represented through the movements and interactions of the planets, as well as the progression through the zodiac signs, each marking a different phase or aspect of life. In Tarot, the sequence of the Major Arcana cards illustrates a journey of personal development and transformation, from the naivety and potential of The Fool to the completion and wholeness of The World. This focus on cycles and transitions highlights the ever-changing nature of life and the continuous process of growth and evolution.

Astrology and tarot operate on both personal and universal levels, offering insights into individual experiences while also tapping into broader, more universal themes. In astrology, an individual's birth chart is a unique snapshot of the celestial bodies at birth, reflecting distinct personal traits and life paths. Similarly, in tarot, while each card carries a general meaning, its interpretation can vary widely based on the querent's circumstances and the specific context of the reading. This dual nature allows both practices to provide tailored guidance to individuals while resonating with universal human experiences and emotions.

By integrating the wisdom of astrology with the symbolism of tarot, practitioners can access a more holistic understanding of themselves and the world around them. Combining planetary influences, elemental energies, and archetypal imagery creates a rich tapestry of meaning, offering a multifaceted approach to personal exploration and insight. This synergy between astrology and tarot not only deepens the practice of each but also provides a comprehensive framework for navigating the complexities of human experiences and relationships. This integrated approach allows for a profound exploration of the self and the universe, where the movements of the planets and the symbolism of the tarot cards interweave to create a narrative that is both deeply personal and universally relevant.

This blending of astrology and tarot extends beyond mere interpretation; it invites a transformative journey of self-awareness and understanding. In astrology, transits and progressions offer insights into the evolving dynamics of one's life, reflecting periods of challenge, growth, and opportunity. Similarly, in tarot, the progression of the cards in a reading can mirror the querent's life journey, highlighting potential obstacles, influences, and outcomes. This dynamic interplay between the celestial and the symbolic provides a powerful tool for navigating life's ebbs and flows, helping individuals to align with their most profound truths and potentials.

Moreover, astrology and tarot serve as gateways to the collective unconscious, drawing upon shared human experiences and archetypes that transcend individual differences. Through their rich symbolism, they tap into the collective myths, stories, and beliefs that shape our understanding of the world. This communal dimension adds depth and universality to personal readings, allowing individuals to connect with broader themes and patterns that resonate across cultures and time.

In contemporary practice, the integration of astrology and tarot is often seen in creating personalized readings and horoscopes, where astrological insights are combined with tarot symbolism to offer guidance tailored to the individual's astrological makeup. This approach not only personalizes the experience but also provides a more nuanced and comprehensive perspective, taking into account the complexities of one's astrological chart and life circumstances.

The fusion of astrology and tarot is also evident in the creative realm, where artists and writers draw inspiration from both systems to create works that explore the human condition. From tarot decks that incorporate astrological symbols to novels and artworks that weave together astrological and tarot imagery, this blending of practices continues to inspire and captivate.

Ultimately, the relationship between astrology and tarot is one of complementarity and enrichment. Each system, with its unique symbols and meanings, enhances the other, offering a richer and more multidimensional perspective on life, the universe, and our place. Whether used for personal reflection, spiritual exploration, or artistic expression, the combined wisdom of astrology and tarot provides a profound and enduring source of insight and inspiration.

Further expiration into this dance between these two disciplines reveals the following:

The Moon, which holds significant importance in astrology, also plays a crucial role in tarot readings. Different moon phases can influence the energy and interpretation of tarot readings, much like how they affect moods and events in astrology. For instance, a full moon might bring heightened emotions and revelations, which can be reflected in more intense and revealing tarot readings. Similarly, a new moon, a time for beginnings and intentions in astrology, can be an opportune moment for tarot readings focused on new ventures or starting afresh. This connection highlights the synchronicity between the lunar cycle's influence in astrology and its resonance in tarot, providing a richer context for readings and interpretations.

Integrating Astrology and Tarot in Practice: In practical terms, many tarot readers incorporate astrological elements into their readings to enhance their depth and accuracy. Knowledge of a querent's astrological sign or chart can inform the interpretation of the cards, allowing for a more personalized and nuanced reading. This integration can be particularly insightful when dealing with complex issues or when trying to understand the underlying dynamics of a situation. By combining the symbolic language of tarot with astrological insights into personality and fate, readers can offer a more comprehensive and tailored experience to those seeking guidance.

Personal Growth and Self-Understanding: At their core, tarot and astrology are tools for personal growth and self-understanding. They provide different yet complementary pathways to exploring one's inner world and life journey. Tarot offers a narrative structure through its cards, allowing individuals to reflect on their life stories and circumstances. Astrology, on the other hand, provides a cosmic perspective, placing individual experiences within the broader context of planetary movements and alignments. Together, these practices offer a holistic approach to self-exploration and personal development, encouraging individuals to delve deeper into their psyche and understand the patterns and cycles that shape their lives.

Exploring these ten aspects of the connection between tarot and astrology reveals a profound and multi-layered relationship. It shows how these two ancient practices, each rich in symbolism and meaning, can complement and enhance each other. Whether used together or separately, tarot and astrology offer valuable insights into the human experience, guiding individuals toward self-discovery and understanding.

Let us delve deeper into the concept of the archetype, especially as presented by JUNG's expensive work in this field.

Delving deeper into the intersection of astrology, tarot, and Jungian archetypes reveals a rich tapestry of symbols and meanings that resonate deeply with the human psyche. Carl Jung, a Swiss psychiatrist and psychoanalyst, introduced the concept of archetypes, which are deeply ingrained universal patterns and images that form part of the collective unconscious. This concept has profound implications for understanding the symbolic language of both astrology and tarot.

Astrology and tarot are deeply intertwined with the concept of archetypes, serving as tools to access and explore the collective unconscious. In astrology, the planets and zodiac signs represent archetypal energies and aspects of the human experience. For instance, the Sun symbolizes the ego and our conscious self, while the Moon represents our inner emotional landscape and instincts. Each zodiac sign, from the pioneering Aries to the compassionate Pisces, embodies an archetypal quality or theme, reflecting different facets of human nature. Similarly, in tarot, the Major Arcana cards are rich with archetypal imagery. The Magician, representing manifestation and creativity, and The High Priestess, symbolizing intuition and mystery, are prime examples of archetypal figures that resonate with Jung's concepts.

The four elements in astrology and tarot – Earth, Water, Air, and Fire – align with Jung's archetypes by representing fundamental human traits and motivations. In astrology, these elements categorize the zodiac signs into groups that share common characteristics, such as the emotional and intuitive nature of Water signs or the intellectual and communicative qualities of Air signs. In tarot, the suits of the Minor Arcana correspond to these elements and imbue the cards with similar attributes. For instance, the suit of Cups (Water) deals with emotional and relational aspects, while the suit of Swords (Air) often concerns thought and communication. These elemental associations provide a framework for understanding and interpreting the diverse aspects of human experience through both practices.

The planetary correspondences in tarot add another layer of archetypal depth. Many tarot cards are associated with specific planets in astrology, each embodying an archetypal energy. For instance, The Hermit card, often linked with Mercury, reflects the seeker archetype or the wise older man, echoing Jung's notion of archetypes as primordial, universal symbols. Understanding these planetary links in tarot enhances reading depth, providing insights rooted in the collective unconscious and shared human experiences.

In many tarot decks, the Major Arcana cards are associated with zodiac signs, establishing a direct connection with astrological archetypes. This association allows for an enriched interpretation of the cards through an astrological lens. For example, The Emperor card, often connected with Aries, embodies the archetype of the ruler or father figure, reflecting themes of authority, structure, and leadership. These astrological associations bring a greater depth to tarot readings, intertwining the archetypal imagery of the cards with the symbolic language of the stars.

Astrology and tarot, as reflective tools, align closely with Jung's concept of individuation – the process of becoming aware of oneself and achieving a sense of wholeness. Both practices offer a means to explore the subconscious and bring to light the various facets of the self, including those that are not immediately conscious. This exploration can aid in personal development and self-understanding, helping individuals to navigate their life paths with greater awareness and insight.

The emphasis on cycles and transitions in astrology and tarot resonates with Jung's view of life as a series of developmental stages and transformations. In astrology, the progression through the zodiac signs and the planetary cycles reflects the ongoing evolution of the self. In tarot, the narrative arc of the Major Arcana, from The Fool to The World, symbolizes a journey of self-discovery and personal growth, mirroring the process of individuation.

Astrology and tarot function on personal and universal levels, offering insights into individual experiences while tapping into broader archetypal themes. An individual's astrological birth chart uniquely combines planetary placements, reflecting unique strengths, challenges, and life lessons. Similarly, in a tarot reading, while each card has a general archetypal meaning, its interpretation is influenced by the querent's situation and the specific question at hand. This personalization allows astrology and tarot to speak directly to individuals and connect them to universal human experiences.

Integrating astrology and tarot with Jungian psychology provides a profound framework for exploring the deeper aspects of the psyche. By combining the archetypal symbolism of the tarot cards with the astrological understanding of planetary and zodiacal energies, practitioners can access a rich insight into the human condition. This approach not only deepens the interpretive power of both practices but also offers a pathway for personal growth and self-realization, reflecting Jung's emphasis on the transformative power of engaging with the unconscious and its symbols.

Moon, which holds significant importance in astrology, also plays a crucial role in tarot readings. Different moon phases can influence the energy and interpretation of tarot readings, much like how they affect moods and events in astrology. For instance, a full moon might bring heightened emotions and revelations, which can be reflected in more intense and revealing tarot readings. Similarly, a new moon, a time for beginnings and intentions in astrology, can be an opportune moment for tarot readings focused on new ventures or starting afresh. This connection highlights the synchronicity between the lunar cycle's influence in astrology and its resonance in tarot, providing a richer context for readings and interpretations.

Integrating Astrology and Tarot in Practice: In practical terms, many tarot readers incorporate astrological elements into their readings to enhance their depth and accuracy. Knowledge of a querent's astrological sign or chart can inform the interpretation of the cards, allowing for a more personalized and nuanced reading. This integration can be particularly insightful when dealing with complex issues or when trying to understand the underlying dynamics of a situation. By combining the symbolic language of tarot with astrological insights into personality and fate, readers can offer a more comprehensive and tailored experience to those seeking guidance.

Personal Growth and Self-Understanding: At their core, tarot and astrology are tools for personal growth and self-understanding. They provide different yet complementary pathways to exploring one's inner world and life journey. Tarot offers a narrative structure through its cards, allowing individuals to reflect on their life stories and circumstances. Astrology, on the other hand, provides a cosmic perspective, placing individual experiences within the broader context of planetary movements and alignments. Together, these practices offer a holistic approach to self-exploration and personal development, encouraging individuals to delve deeper into their psyche and understand the patterns and cycles that shape their lives.

Exploring these ten aspects of the connection between tarot and astrology reveals a profound and multi-layered relationship. It shows how these two ancient practices, each rich in symbolism and meaning, can complement and enhance each other. Whether used together or separately, tarot and astrology offer valuable insights into the human experience, guiding individuals toward self-discovery and understanding.

Chapter 4: Tarot and Psychology

Explore the psychological aspects of tarot, particularly its use in self-reflection, therapy, and personal growth, drawing on Jungian psychology and other theories.

Tarot and psychology intertwine in fascinating ways, mainly through the lens of Jungian psychology and other psychological theories. The use of tarot in self-reflection, therapy, and personal growth offers a unique perspective on the human psyche and personal development.

The integration of tarot into psychological practices primarily stems from its rich symbolism, which resonates with Carl Jung's concept of archetypes. Jungian psychology posits that archetypes are universal, archaic symbols and images derived from the collective unconscious. Tarot cards, with their intricate and symbolic imagery, tap into these archetypes, allowing individuals to explore their subconscious and gain insights into their inner world.

Tarot cards serve as reflective tools, mirroring the individual's thoughts, feelings, and experiences. When used in a therapeutic context, tarot can help individuals clarify their situations, unravel complex emotions, and explore potential paths forward. This reflective process encourages introspection and self-awareness, critical components in personal growth and psychological healing.

The narrative aspect of tarot readings aligns with narrative therapy, a therapeutic approach that emphasizes the stories we tell about our lives. Tarot readings can help individuals reframe their narratives, recognize recurring patterns, and understand their role in shaping their life stories. This process can be empowering, placing the individual at the center of their narrative.

Tarot's emphasis on intuition is another point of convergence with psychology. Intuitive readings encourage individuals to trust their inner voice and wisdom. This process can be particularly therapeutic, as it reinforces the individual's ability to guide their journey and make decisions that align with their true self.

The Major and Minor Arcana in tarot decks correspond to different aspects of the human experience. The Major Arcana deals with major life themes and lessons, while the Minor Arcana reflects day-to-day events. This distinction mirrors psychological concepts of overarching life themes versus everyday experiences, allowing for a comprehensive exploration of an individual's life.

Tarot can also be a tool for exploring shadow aspects of the personality, a concept introduced by Jung. The shadow represents the repressed or ignored parts of oneself. Certain tarot cards can bring these aspects to light, allowing individuals to confront and integrate these hidden parts of themselves.

The imagery in tarot decks often includes symbols of transformation and rebirth, such as the Death card, which symbolizes the end of a cycle and the start of a new one. This symbolism aligns with psychological concepts of change, growth, and transformation, making tarot a relevant tool for exploring these themes in therapy and self-reflection.

Tarot readings can facilitate the exploration of relationship dynamics and interpersonal issues. The cards can reflect different roles, patterns, and dynamics that one might experience in relationships, providing insights that can be useful in counseling and personal development.

The use of tarot in therapy is not about predicting the future but exploring possible outcomes and paths. This approach aligns with cognitive-behavioral therapy, which explores thoughts, beliefs, and attitudes to understand and change behavior. Tarot can complement this process, offering a visual and symbolic way to examine and challenge these cognitive patterns.

In summary, using tarot in the context of psychology offers a unique blend of symbolism, narrative, and self-exploration. Whether used in therapy or personal growth, tarot provides a rich and multifaceted tool for delving into the human psyche, facilitating self-awareness, and fostering personal development. The convergence of tarot and psychology reveals the depth and versatility of tarot as a tool for exploring the complexities of the mind and the nuances of the human experience

Chapter 5: Practical Tips for Tarot Reading

Offer practical advice for conducting tarot readings, such as creating the right environment, grounding oneself, ethical consideration, setting the physical environment that might be most conducive, arranging furniture, shoes, choice of colors, pillows, etc.

Mementos that resonate with the reader's journey or the themes commonly explored in readings. These items not only add a personal touch but also create a sense of connection and depth to the reading process. They can act as focal points or tools for meditation, helping both the reader and the querent to connect more deeply with the spiritual dimensions of the tarot. Elements like a special cloth for laying out tarot cards, symbolic statues, or artwork can also enrich the environment, making the space feel more sacred and attuned to the mystical nature of tarot readings.

The arrangement and selection of furniture in the tarot reading space should not only be about comfort but also about creating an environment conducive to openness and connection. Chairs or seating should be arranged to facilitate a sense of equality and mutual respect between the reader and the querent. A round or oval table can symbolize unity and continuity, enhancing energy flow during the reading. The furniture should also be chosen with mindfulness to its material and form, with natural materials like wood being preferable for their grounding qualities.

Plants can be an excellent addition to a tarot reading space. They bring in natural energy and help to purify the air, creating a more vibrant and alive environment. Plants can also have a calming effect, helping to ease anxiety and promote a relaxed state of mind. Choosing plants that are easy to care for and that thrive in the specific conditions of your reading space is essential, as healthy, flourishing plants contribute positively to the atmosphere.

Music or ambient sounds can further enhance the tarot reading experience. Soft, soothing music or natural sounds like flowing water or birdsong can help set a serene and contemplative mood. It's essential to select sounds that are not too distracting or overpowering but serve as a gentle backdrop to the reading process, aiding in concentration and relaxation.

Temperature and air quality are often overlooked aspects of creating a conducive tarot reading environment. The space should be comfortable, neither too hot nor too cold, allowing the reader and the querent to stay focused and at ease. Good ventilation is also crucial, as a fresh and airy room helps maintain clear and positive energy. If the room feels stuffy or stagnant, it can negatively impact the reading quality.

Aromatherapy can be a powerful tool in a tarot reading space. Scents like lavender, sage, or frankincense can be calming and cleansing, helping to set the mood and clear the space of negative energy. However, it's essential to be mindful of any allergies or sensitivities, either your own or those of your querents. Aromatherapy should enhance the experience, not cause discomfort.

Creating a sacred space for tarot reading involves more than just physical arrangements; it's about cultivating an atmosphere that resonates with spirituality, introspection, and connection. By paying attention to these various aspects, from the physical setting to the more subtle elements like scent and sound, you can create a tarot reading environment that is not only conducive to insightful readings but also a sanctuary for spiritual exploration and growth.

Ethics and responsibility are paramount in tarot reading, as they ensure a respectful, safe, and insightful experience for both the reader and the querent. Navigating the delicate balance between offering guidance and maintaining a moral and ethical stance is crucial in this practice.

A tarot reader holds a position of trust and influence, making it vital to approach each reading with honesty and integrity. This includes being truthful about what the cards reveal avoiding the embellishment of interpretations to make them more appealing or dramatic. It's important to acknowledge that tarot readings are not infallible future predictions but insights and guidance based on the cards drawn.

Maintaining client confidentiality is a fundamental ethical responsibility for tarot readers. As in any therapeutic or counseling profession, the information shared during a tarot reading should be confidential. This trust forms the foundation of the reader-querent relationship and ensures that the querent feels safe to share personal and potentially sensitive information.

Dealing with sensitive topics requires tact, compassion, and, sometimes, restraint. A tarot reader should be prepared to encounter complex and challenging situations. It's essential to approach these readings empathetically, offering supportive and constructive interpretations rather than alarming or overly directive.

Establishing clear boundaries is also a critical ethical consideration. This includes limiting the type of questions appropriate for a tarot reading, such as avoiding predictions about health, legal matters, or financial investments. A responsible tarot reader should know when to refer a querent to a qualified professional in areas outside their expertise.

A specific code of ethics can be a valuable guide for tarot readers. This could include respecting the autonomy and decision-making power of the querent, committing to non-judgmental and unbiased readings, and continually improving one's skills and understanding of tarot.

Being mindful of the language used during readings is an important ethical consideration. Words have power, and how a reading is delivered can significantly impact the querent. It's crucial to choose words that are empowering and hopeful rather than fear-inducing or deterministic.

Handling predictions responsibly is a crucial aspect of ethical tarot reading. While tarot can offer insights into potential future outcomes, it's important to emphasize the querent's free will and that the future is not set in stone. Readers should avoid making absolute statements about the future, instead framing insights to highlight possibilities and choices.

An ethical tarot reader should always prioritize the well-being of the querent. This means conducting readings in a manner that is respectful, encouraging, and focused on the querent's growth and self-discovery. The reader's role is to offer insights that can aid the querent in their journey, not to dictate or control their path.

Finally, ongoing self-reflection and assessment of one's motives and practices as a tarot reader are crucial. This involves continually questioning and evaluating how one's readings are conducted, their impact on querent, and how to improve and refine the practice ethically. Being a tarot reader is guiding others and continuously learning and growing oneself.

In some cases, depending on the nature of the tarot reading sessions, it might be beneficial for a reader to explore becoming an ordained minister. In several states in the United States, one can apply online to become an ordained minister. This status can allow the tarot reader to hold sessions with a level of confidentiality akin to that of a pastoral counselor. It adds a layer of trust and ethical responsibility to the reader's role, emphasizing the sacredness and seriousness with which the practice should be approached.

In summary, ethics and responsibility in tarot reading encompass a range of practices and considerations, from maintaining confidentiality to handling sensitive topics with care. By adhering to a solid ethical code and approaching readings with respect, integrity, and empathy, tarot readers can provide valuable, insightful, and empowering experiences for their querents. These principles ensure that tarot reading remains a respected and valuable practice focused on guidance, personal growth, and self-awareness.

Chapter 6: Exploring the Concept of the Tarot in Greater Length

Addressing frequently asked tarot questions is essential for demystifying this practice, especially for beginners or those with a budding interest. It helps dispel myths and clarifies the tarot's nature and usage.

"What exactly is tarot?" is a common starting point for many. Tarot is a deck of 78 cards, each rich in symbolism and storytelling potential. It comprises the Major and Minor Arcana, with the Major Arcana depicting significant life lessons and themes and the Minor Arcana reflecting day-to-day events. The imagery in these cards ranges from classical and historical to modern and abstract, making tarot a versatile tool for personal reflection and understanding.

Another question often posed is, "Do you need psychic abilities to read tarot cards?" The answer lies more in intuition than in psychic powers. While some readers may possess psychic abilities, tarot reading mainly hinges on the reader's capacity to interpret the symbols and narratives on the cards intuitively and how these relate to everyday life or specific situations. It's a skill that combines empathy, symbolism understanding, and a bit of narrative creativity.

A common misconception about tarot is its use in predicting the future. While tarot can offer insight into possible futures, it is more about exploring potential paths and guiding decision-making. Tarot readings should be viewed as a tool to help understand complex situations and to contemplate different approaches rather than as a means to predict unchangeable future events.

For beginners, a frequent query is, "How do I start reading tarot cards?" Beginning with a deck that resonates with you is crucial.

Learning the meanings of the cards is just the first step. Engaging with the cards through daily practice, reflective journaling, and even incorporating them into meditation can deepen your understanding. Many find it beneficial to join tarot communities or groups to share insights and learn from others.

The question of safety often arises: "Is tarot reading safe?" Yes, when approached correctly. Tarot is a tool for self-discovery and contemplation. It's crucial to approach readings with an open yet grounded mindset and to use the insights as guidance rather than absolute truths. It's also vital to come tarot ethically, especially when reading for others, to avoid creating dependencies or instilling fear.

"Can tarot aid in decision-making?" is another joint inquiry. Tarot can be particularly useful in decision-making processes as it helps illuminate different facets of a situation. It encourages exploring various perspectives, often bringing to light aspects that might have been overlooked. It's a means to foster introspection and consider the broader implications of choices.

Regarding the rules of tarot reading, while traditional meanings provide a foundation, the practice is inherently personal and subjective. Tarot reading is more art than science, allowing various interpretations and approaches. The symbolism in the cards can evoke different responses based on the reader's and querent's experiences and perspectives.

Reading tarot for oneself is a frequently explored topic. Personal tarot readings can be deeply insightful, offering a reflective space to explore one's thoughts, feelings, and the broader journey of life. It requires honesty and openness with oneself and can sometimes be challenging, as it may bring to light uncomfortable truths or hidden thoughts.

The relationship between tarot and specific religions or belief systems is often questioned. Tarot is a spiritual tool but not inherently religious. Its practice is separate from religious doctrines, making it accessible to people of various beliefs and backgrounds. The symbols in tarot may draw from a wide range of cultural and spiritual sources, reflecting its universal applicability.

Lastly, the accuracy of tarot readings is a topic of much interest. The accuracy can vary, influenced by the reader's skill and the querent's receptiveness to the reading. Tarot readings should be seen as a source of guidance and a way to gain new perspectives. They offer a reflective mirror to our inner world and situations rather than a definitive prediction of future events.

These expanded answers aim to provide a deeper understanding of tarot reading, helping beginners and the curious navigate this intriguing and reflective practice. Each aspect of tarot, from its history to its application, reveals its role not just as a divinatory tool but as a rich, symbolic medium for personal growth and understanding.

Exploring the world of tarot offers endless opportunities for learning and growth. For those keen on deepening their understanding and practice of tarot, many resources are available, ranging from traditional to modern platforms.

Books on tarot are foundational resources. Titles such as "Tarot for Your Self" by Mary K. Greer offer a unique approach to personal exploration. At the same time, "The Complete Book of Tarot Reversals" by the same author is invaluable for understanding the significance of reversed cards. For a deep dive into the psychological aspects of tarot, "Tarot and Psychology: Spectrums of Possibility" by Arthur Rosengarten blends tarot practice with psychological concepts.

Online resources are plentiful and diverse. The Tarot School website is an excellent place for comprehensive learning, offering courses, audio lessons, and certificates. For those who prefer a more interactive online learning experience, The Tarot School hosts an annual Tarot Readers Studio, a conference for tarot enthusiasts.

Dedicated tarot courses offer structured learning experiences. Websites like The Hermetic Tarot School provide in-depth courses on various aspects of tarot, including symbolism, reading techniques, and historical contexts. These courses often come with personalized feedback, enhancing the learning experience.

YouTube channels dedicated to tarot offer visual and interactive content. Channels like "Ethony" provide educational content and insights into different tarot decks, reading techniques, and the spiritual aspects of tarot. These channels can benefit visual learners and those seeking practical tarot reading demonstrations.

Tarot communities on social media platforms are thriving hubs for exchange and learning. Instagram accounts like @tarotprose share daily card interpretations and insights, while Reddit's r/tarot community offers a platform for discussion, question-and-answer sessions, and sharing reading experiences.

Mobile apps for tarot learning and practice are increasingly popular. The Fool's Dog offers a range of tarot apps for different decks, with detailed interpretations and journaling features. These apps are convenient for learning and practicing tarot on the go.

Podcasts about tarot provide insights and discussions for auditory learners. "Strange Magic" is a podcast that delves into tarot card meanings, mythological tales, and artistic interpretations, offering a deeper understanding of the cards in a relaxed, conversational format.

Local tarot classes and workshops, often available in metaphysical stores or spiritual centers, offer hands-on learning experiences. These classes provide direct guidance from experienced tarot practitioners and the opportunity to practice readings in a supportive environment.

For an immersive experience, tarot-focused retreats and festivals, like the Reader's Studio in New York or the Omega Tarot Conference, bring together tarot enthusiasts from around the world. These events are ideal for networking, learning from seasoned tarot professionals, and immersing oneself in tarot study.

In addition to these resources, tarot journals and guided workbooks can significantly enhance one's tarot journey. Books like "Tarot Journaling" by Corrine Kenner guide users through keeping a detailed tarot journal, which can be a transformative tool for personal growth and improving reading skills.

These resources collectively form a comprehensive guide for anyone interested in exploring tarot, offering various ways to engage with and learn from the rich tradition of tarot reading. From books to digital platforms, each resource provides unique insights and learning opportunities, catering to diverse preferences and learning styles in the world of tarot.

Please see the last section of this book, which gives a comprehensive listing of referrals that may be helpful to the reader.

Chapter 7: The Tarot Cards

The Major Arcana

Fool

"The Fool," often numbered as zero or placed at the beginning of the Major Arcana in tarot decks, is a card rich with symbolism and deep psychological significance. In its most fundamental interpretation, The Fool represents new beginnings, potential, and a journey into the unknown. This card is characterized by a figure stepping into the world with a sense of innocence and adventure, often depicted on the brink of a precipice, symbolizing the leap of faith and the initiation of a journey. The Fool carries a small sack, representing untapped knowledge and potential, and is accompanied by a dog, symbolizing loyalty and protection. This imagery resonates with the Jungian concept of the archetype of 'The Hero' embarking on a journey – a narrative of adventure and transformation.

Psychologically, The Fool embodies the pure state of mind, unburdened by past experiences and open to all possibilities – akin to the Jungian idea of the 'child archetype.' This card signifies the spirit of exploration, encouraging the querent to embrace new experiences with an open heart and mind. The Fool's apparent lack of concern as he steps toward the unknown can be interpreted as a message to trust the process and embrace uncertainty. In a reading, The Fool may suggest that it is time to take a risk or embark on a new adventure without preconceptions or fears of failure.

The Fool can also represent the beginning of a spiritual or personal journey that involves self-discovery and growth. This journey might require leaving behind old beliefs and entering a phase of learning and experience, indicative of the Jungian individuation process. The card's energy is not just about external exploration but also about exploring the inner self, searching for one's true identity and purpose.

When The Fool appears reversed in a tarot reading, it may signify recklessness, naive impulsiveness, or folly. The reversed position can suggest that the querent is acting without forethought, potentially leading to harmful consequences. It can also indicate a reluctance to start a new journey due to fear or uncertainty or a feeling of being directionless.

Through the lens of Carl Jung's theories, The Fool can be seen as embodying the 'Trickster' archetype. The Trickster is often associated with breaking the rules, challenging conventions, and introducing chaos into the order, mirroring The Fool's disregard for conventional paths. However, like the Trickster, The Fool's actions can lead to positive change and transformation, shaking up the status quo to create new opportunities for growth and learning.

"The Fool," in Jungian terms, is an emblem of the potential for transformation and the adventurous spirit within every individual. It invites an exploration of the unknown and a willingness to step into new experiences. It reflects the ever-present possibility of a fresh start and the importance of maintaining an open, curious, and flexible attitude throughout life's journey.

Expanding on the analysis of "The Fool" tarot card from a psychological and symbolic perspective, additional insights can be drawn:

The Symbol of the Journey: "The Fool" as a symbol for life's journey is not just about physical travel but also a metaphor for the inner journey of self-discovery and personal development. This card can represent the Jungian idea of the 'path of individuation,' where one embarks on a quest for self-actualization, seeking to integrate different aspects of the psyche.

Threshold of Transformation: The Fool standing at the edge of a cliff signifies physical risk and the threshold between the known and the unknown. In Jungian terms, this can be seen as the boundary between the conscious and unconscious mind, where stepping off the ledge represents a dive into the deeper aspects of the self.

The Role of the Shadow: The dog accompanying The Fool could be interpreted as a manifestation of the shadow self in Jungian psychology. The shadow represents the parts of our personality that we repress or deny. In the tarot, the dog can symbolize instincts or hidden aspects of the self that accompany us on our journey, even if not fully acknowledged.

The Collective Unconscious: The imagery and symbols in The Fool card resonate with the collective unconscious, a concept in Jungian psychology that refers to the part of the unconscious mind derived from ancestral memory and experience and is expected of all humankind. The archetypal themes in The Fool—adventure, beginnings, innocence—speak to universal experiences and emotions.

The Anima/Animus: Depending on the querent's gender and personal journey, The Fool can also embody the Anima or Animus – the opposite gender aspects within the psyche. This represents the integration and acknowledgment of the masculine and feminine elements within oneself, which is crucial for psychological wholeness.

The Fool's Journey as a Narrative: The Fool's journey through the tarot's Major Arcana can be likened to the monomyth or the hero's journey. Each card represents a stage in this journey, with The Fool symbolizing the hero at the outset, naive and untested but open to all possibilities.

Magician

"The Magician," often numbered as the first card in the Major Arcana of tarot decks, is a symbol of manifestation, resourcefulness, and power. This card typically features a figure standing before a table with various symbolic objects representing the four suits of the tarot (wands, cups, swords, pentacles), signifying the elements of the natural world and the abilities of the Magician to manipulate them. Above his head is the symbol of infinity, indicating endless potential and the eternal nature of energy and matter.

Psychologically, The Magician symbolizes the conscious mind's ability to harness the power of the subconscious. In Jungian terms, this card can represent the process of bringing the unconscious into consciousness, thus achieving mastery over one's thoughts and environment. This aligns with the concept of the 'self' in Jungian psychology – the unification and integration of the conscious and unconscious aspects of the psyche. The Magician's channeling of the elements can be seen as an allegory for using one's skills and resources to achieve goals and realize intentions.

The Magician's posture, with one hand pointing to the sky and the other to the ground, symbolizes the axiom "as above, so below," reflecting the Jungian idea that the external world is a reflection of the internal world. This suggests that change and manifestation begin within before they can be externalized. The Magician thus calls on the querent to recognize their potential for self-mastery and creation.

When The Magician appears reversed in a reading, it can indicate misuse of one's abilities, such as manipulation or deceit. It may also suggest self-doubt, where the individual's potential is hindered by a lack of confidence in their skills or not fully realizing their power.

Through the lens of Carl Jung's theories, The Magician can be seen as representing the 'animus' in women or the 'persona' in both men and women – the outward face we present to the world, which can either be authentic or a mask to hide our true nature. The Magician encourages the integration of these aspects, urging the individual to use their persona effectively without losing touch with their authentic self.

"The Magician" is a powerful symbol of the potential within each person to harness their inner resources, using knowledge and tools available to them. It speaks to the importance of belief in oneself and the ability to turn possibilities into realities, a fundamental aspect of human psychology and the journey toward wholeness and self-actualization.

Expanding on the analysis of "The Magician" tarot card from a psychological and symbolic perspective, additional insights can be drawn:

The Symbol of Transformation: "The Magician" is a powerful symbol of transformation and transmutation, echoing the alchemical process of turning lead into gold. This process symbolizes the transformation of base instincts and desires into higher spiritual aims, aligning with the Jungian individuation process.

The Role of Willpower and Intention: The Magician highlights the importance of willpower and intention in the Jungian therapeutic process. It suggests that the conscious direction of will is crucial for personal growth and the realization of the self.

The Collective Unconscious: The imagery and symbols in The Magician card resonate with the collective unconscious, containing archetypal elements common to all human experiences. The tools on the Magician's table represent different aspects of life and the human experience, accessible to all through the collective unconscious.

The Anima/Animus: The Magician, in specific readings, can also represent the Anima or Animus – the inner feminine in men or the inner masculine in women. This highlights the Magician's role in balancing and integrating these aspects within the psyche for harmony and completeness.

The Magician's Journey as a Narrative: The Magician's journey in the tarot can be seen as a metaphor for the individual's journey through life. Each tool and element represents different stages and challenges, with The Magician symbolizing the ability to navigate these successfully.

"The Magician" thus serves as a reminder of the power inherent in each individual to shape their reality and destiny. It is a call to action to use one's abilities and resources wisely and intentionally, vital for personal empowerment and psychological development.

The High Priestess

"The High Priestess," often numbered as the second card in the Major Arcana of tarot decks, embodies deep intuition, mystery, and a connection to the subconscious. She is typically depicted sitting between two pillars, symbolizing the threshold between the conscious and subconscious worlds. Holding a scroll or a book, she represents the keeper of hidden knowledge and esoteric wisdom. The lunar crescent, frequently seen at her feet or adorning her head, ties her to the feminine, intuitive, and cyclical nature of the moon, reflecting the unconscious mind's profound depths.

Psychologically, The High Priestess bridges the unseen, urging a deeper understanding and trust in one's inner voice. This card in a reading suggests delving into the subconscious, uncovering hidden truths, and relying on intuition. She personifies the Jungian 'anima,' the feminine aspect within the male psyche, promoting the harmonious integration of intuition and inner wisdom within one's personality.

The High Priestess's composed and serene presence invites contemplation and introspection. She reminds us that true wisdom often emerges from within and that quiet reflection can yield significant insights. She indicates a period ripe for revelations and more profound understanding, where the unseen becomes visible, and the unspoken finds a voice.

In her reversed position, The High Priestess may signal ignored intuition, hidden motives, or suppressed inner truths. This suggests a disconnection from the inner self, leading to confusion or misalignment with one's authentic path.

Through Carl Jung's perspectives, The High Priestess also symbolizes the collective unconscious, holding the keys to profound, universal truths. Her presence in a reading can bring forth archetypal images and ideas from the collective unconscious, offering deep insights and guiding the individual toward greater self-awareness.

"The High Priestess" stands as a symbol of the unexplored and mystical facets of the psyche. She encourages delving into the inner self, trusting intuition, and acknowledging the deeper layers of personality and experience. Her presence suggests much to be learned from what lies beneath the surface of conscious thought.

Gateway to Inner Mysteries: The High Priestess serves as a gateway to the inner mysteries of the psyche, encouraging exploration of the deeper realms of the self. She invites a journey into the world of dreams, symbols, and hidden desires, where much of our true motivations and insights reside.

Connection to the Divine Feminine: The High Priestess often symbolizes the divine feminine principle, representing intuition, receptivity, and the nurturing aspects of the psyche. She encourages balancing the masculine and feminine energies within oneself, regardless of gender, to achieve a more holistic perspective.

The Veil of Awareness: The veil behind The High Priestess signifies the thin barrier between the known and unknown. It reminds us that beyond the veil lies a rich world of intuitive knowledge that one can access through meditation and introspection.

The High Priestess and Shadow Work: In Jungian psychology, facing the shadow self is crucial for personal growth. The High Priestess encourages this journey, guiding the individual to confront and integrate the shadow aspects to achieve psychological wholeness.

The High Priestess as a Reflective Mirror: She acts as a mirror, reflecting the hidden depths of our psyche. In a reading, she asks us to look inward, to understand our true motivations, fears, and desires, and to use this understanding for personal growth and enlightenment.

"The High Priestess" thus is a profound reminder of the importance of inner exploration and intuition. She encourages a deeper engagement with the inner self, emphasizing intuition as a guide in self-discovery, personal growth, and understanding the deeper layers of one's existence.

Empress

"The Empress," commonly the third card in the Major Arcana of tarot decks, is a powerful symbol of fertility, creativity, and nurturing. She is often depicted in a lush, verdant landscape, embodying the richness of Mother Earth. The Empress is frequently shown with fertility symbols like pomegranates or wheat and may appear pregnant, underscoring her role as a life-giver and caretaker. Her representation as a regal figure in nature highlights her connection to abundance and the nurturing of life.

In psychological terms, The Empress embodies the nurturing facet of the psyche. She signifies the capacity for nurturing, empathy, love, and compassion. Her presence in reading encourages embracing and expressing these qualities, signaling growth and development in relationships, creative projects, or personal pursuits. She resonates with the Jungian 'Great Mother' archetype, signifying maternal instincts, protection, and unconditional love.

The Empress's appearance in a tarot spread signifies a period of abundance, sensuality, and connection with nature. She invites appreciation for beauty, comfort, and life's sensual aspects, signaling a time to nurture oneself and others and to relish life's pleasures.

When reversed, The Empress may point to issues in nurturing dynamics, such as neglect or overprotectiveness. It may call attention to the need for self-care or to address imbalances in giving and receiving care and affection.

Through the lens of Carl Jung's theories, The Empress represents the collective unconscious's fertility aspect, the source of creativity, ideas, and life. She embodies the life-giving and sustaining energy of the feminine principle.

"The Empress" symbolizes nurturing power and creativity. She personifies the essence of motherhood, fertility, and abundance, urging a deeper bond with nature and the nurturing self. Her card suggests that embracing these qualities can enrich one's life experiences.

Earthly Connection: The Empress emphasizes our deep connection to Earth and nature, underlining the nurturing power and sustenance the environment provides. She advocates for a balanced, respectful relationship with nature, celebrating its beauty and abundance.

Importance of Feminine Energy: The Empress highlights the value of feminine energy, characterized by receptivity, empathy, and nurturing qualities. She calls for a balance of strength and gentleness, encouraging the integration of these aspects regardless of gender.

Creative and Artistic Flourishing: The Empress is a beacon for creativity and artistic expression. Her card is a reminder to engage with one's creative abilities, finding joy and fulfillment in artistic pursuits.

Emotional Wealth: The Empress is associated with emotional richness and the ability to give and receive love. She fosters a sense of open-heartedness and emotional generosity, laying the foundation for relationships based on mutual nurturing and respect.

Guidance for Emotional and Self-Care Balance: In readings, The Empress is a guide to balancing caring for others with self-nurturing. She highlights the necessity of self-care to nurture others effectively.

Symbol of Growth and Prosperity: The Empress represents not just physical growth and prosperity but also personal and spiritual growth. She suggests that growth often comes from a place of love, care, and emotional fulfillment.

The Empress as an Inspirational Muse: Her presence in a spread can be seen as an inspiration for artistic and creative endeavors, where she serves as a muse, encouraging the exploration of beauty and art in all forms.

The Empress in Relationship Readings: In relationship contexts, The Empress can symbolize a nurturing, supportive partner or the growth of a relationship. She encourages a loving, caring approach in interactions with others.

"The Empress" thus reminds us of the nurturing and creative forces within and around us. She encourages an embracing of nurturing qualities, the pursuit of creative endeavors, and the fostering of deep, meaningful connections, enhancing emotional, personal, and environmental well-being.

"The Empress," commonly the third card in the Major Arcana of tarot decks, is a powerful symbol of fertility, creativity, and nurturing. She is often depicted in a lush, verdant landscape, embodying the richness of Mother Earth. The Empress is frequently shown with fertility symbols like pomegranates or wheat and may appear pregnant, underscoring her role as a life-giver and caretaker. Her representation as a regal figure in nature highlights her connection to abundance and the nurturing of life.

In psychological terms, The Empress embodies the nurturing facet of the psyche. She signifies the capacity for nurturing, empathy, love, and compassion. Her presence in reading encourages embracing and expressing these qualities, signaling growth and development in relationships, creative projects, or personal pursuits. She resonates with the Jungian 'Great Mother' archetype, signifying maternal instincts, protection, and unconditional love.

The Empress's appearance in a tarot spread signifies a period of abundance, sensuality, and connection with nature. She invites appreciation for beauty, comfort, and life's sensual aspects, signaling a time to nurture oneself and others and to relish life's pleasures.

When reversed, The Empress may point to issues in nurturing dynamics, such as neglect or overprotectiveness. It may call attention to the need for self-care or to address imbalances in giving and receiving care and affection.

Through the lens of Carl Jung's theories, The Empress represents the collective unconscious's fertility aspect, the source of creativity, ideas, and life. She embodies the life-giving and sustaining energy of the feminine principle.

"The Empress" symbolizes nurturing power and creativity. She personifies the essence of motherhood, fertility, and abundance, urging a deeper bond with nature and the nurturing self. Her card suggests that embracing these qualities can enrich one's life experiences.

Earthly Connection: The Empress emphasizes our deep connection to Earth and nature, underlining the nurturing power and sustenance the environment provides. She advocates for a balanced, respectful relationship with nature, celebrating its beauty and abundance.

Importance of Feminine Energy: The Empress highlights the value of feminine energy, characterized by receptivity, empathy, and nurturing qualities. She calls for a balance of strength and gentleness, encouraging the integration of these aspects regardless of gender.

Creative and Artistic Flourishing: The Empress is a beacon for creativity and artistic expression. Her card is a reminder to engage with one's creative abilities, finding joy and fulfillment in artistic pursuits.

Emotional Wealth: The Empress is associated with emotional richness and the ability to give and receive love. She fosters a sense of open-heartedness and emotional generosity, laying the foundation for relationships based on mutual nurturing and respect.

Guidance for Emotional and Self-Care Balance: In readings, The Empress is a guide to balancing caring for others with self-nurturing. She highlights the necessity of self-care to nurture others effectively.

Symbol of Growth and Prosperity: The Empress represents not just physical growth and prosperity but also personal and spiritual growth.

She suggests that growth often comes from a place of love, care, and emotional fulfillment.

The Empress as an Inspirational Muse: Her presence in a spread can be seen as an inspiration for artistic and creative endeavors, where she serves as a muse, encouraging the exploration of beauty and art in all forms.

The Empress in Relationship Readings: In relationship contexts, The Empress can symbolize a nurturing, supportive partner or the growth of a relationship. She encourages a loving, caring approach in interactions with others.

"The Empress" thus reminds us of the nurturing and creative forces within and around us. She encourages an embracing of nurturing qualities, the pursuit of creative endeavors, and the fostering of deep, meaningful connections, enhancing emotional, personal, and environmental well-being.

Emperor

"The Emperor," typically the fourth card in the Major Arcana of tarot decks, represents authority, structure, and control. He is often depicted seated on a throne, symbolizing power and stability. His regal posture and the authoritative look in his eyes reflect his role as a leader and protector. The Emperor is frequently shown with an ankh or orb, a symbol of life and power, and sometimes a scepter, denoting his dominion and governance.

Psychologically, The Emperor embodies the principle of masculine authority and the rational mind. He signifies the capacity for leadership, decision-making, and establishing order and rules. In a reading, The Emperor suggests a period of organization and control, urging the querent to take charge and implement structure in their life. He resonates with the Jungian archetype of the 'Father,' representing discipline, guidance, and protection.

The Emperor's presence in a tarot spread signifies a time for assertiveness and taking the initiative. He encourages the establishment of clear boundaries and the pursuit of goals with determination and pragmatism. His card indicates a phase where leadership and rational thinking are paramount.

When reversed, The Emperor may indicate an abuse of power, rigidity, or over-control. It might suggest a need to loosen the reins and adopt a more flexible approach. The reversed Emperor can also point to a lack of authority or structure in one's life.

Through Carl Jung's theories, The Emperor represents the collective unconscious's aspect of order and rationality. He embodies the structuring element of the psyche, organizing and making sense of the world through logic and reason.

"The Emperor" symbolizes the power of rationality and authority. He personifies leadership, stability, and the structuring of chaos into order, encouraging a disciplined approach to life's challenges. His card suggests that asserting control and structure can lead to success and fulfillment.

Establishment of Order: The Emperor emphasizes the importance of creating order and structure in one's life. He advocates for a systematic, organized approach to achieving objectives.

Masculine Energy and its Expression: The Emperor highlights the value of male energy, characterized by assertiveness, strength, and rationality. He calls for a balance of these qualities, encouraging their positive expression.

Leadership and Responsibility: The Emperor is a symbol of leadership and responsibility. His card suggests taking responsibility for one's actions and decisions and stepping into a leadership role when necessary.

Strategic Thinking and Planning: The Emperor encourages strategic thinking and long-term planning. He suggests that careful planning and rational decision-making are keys to overcoming challenges and achieving goals.

Discipline and Self-Control: The Emperor stands for discipline and self-control. He reminds us that self-discipline is essential for personal growth and achieving ambitions.

The Emperor as a Symbol of Protection: In readings, The Emperor can represent a protective figure or the need for protection in a situation. He suggests creating a safe and stable environment for oneself and others.

Rational Over Emotional Decision-Making: The Emperor advises prioritizing rationality over emotion in decision-making processes, promoting logical analysis and practical solutions.

The Emperor in Career and Business Readings: In career or business contexts, The Emperor can symbolize an influential leader, a structured approach, or the need for solid strategies and plans.

"The Emperor" thus serves as a reminder of the strength found in order, discipline, and rational leadership. He encourages an assertive, structured approach to life's challenges, emphasizing the importance of responsibility, strategic planning, and protection in personal and professional realms.

Hierophant

"The Hierophant," often numbered as the fifth card in the Major Arcana of tarot decks, symbolizes tradition, spiritual wisdom, and conventional beliefs. He is typically depicted as a religious or spiritual leader seated between two pillars of a sacred temple, representing a bridge between heaven and earth. The Hierophant is often shown giving a blessing or holding a key, signifying his role as a mediator of sacred knowledge and a keeper of hidden truths.

Psychologically, The Hierophant embodies the principles of established beliefs and societal norms. He represents the collective consciousness and the acceptance of cultural systems and traditions. In a reading, The Hierophant suggests adherence to conventional beliefs or practices, emphasizing the value of spiritual guidance and traditional wisdom. He resonates with the Jungian archetype of the 'Wise Old Man,' offering knowledge, reflection, and insight.

The Hierophant's presence in a tarot spread signifies a time to honor traditions and seek guidance from established sources. He encourages exploring spiritual or cultural paths and emphasizes the importance of rituals and ceremonies in personal growth and community bonding.

When reversed, The Hierophant may indicate rebellion against conventions, orthodoxy, or a rigid belief system. It might suggest a need to break free from traditional constraints and explore new beliefs or unconventional approaches to spirituality.

Through Carl Jung's theories, The Hierophant represents the collective unconscious's aspect of traditional wisdom and shared beliefs. He embodies the societal structures and norms that shape collective behavior and thought patterns.

"The Hierophant" symbolizes the importance of tradition, spiritual wisdom, and the role of societal norms. He personifies guidance, tradition, and collective knowledge sharing, encouraging a respectful approach to cultural and spiritual practices. His card suggests understanding and integrating traditional wisdom can provide stability and guidance.

Embracing Cultural Heritage: The Hierophant emphasizes the significance of cultural heritage and traditions, encouraging an appreciation and deeper understanding of one's roots and societal values.

Mentorship and Guidance: The Hierophant symbolizes mentorship and guidance, representing figures or institutions that provide learning and direction, especially in spiritual or moral matters.

Rituals and Ceremonies: The Hierophant highlights the role of rituals and ceremonies in human life, stressing their importance in marking significant life events and transitions.

Conformity vs. Individuality: The Hierophant questions the balance between conformity to societal norms and personal individuality, challenging individuals to find harmony between these aspects.

Spiritual Exploration: The Hierophant invites exploration of spiritual paths and religious teachings, suggesting that such journeys can offer profound insights and personal growth.

The Hierophant in Education and Learning: In educational contexts, The Hierophant can symbolize structured learning, traditional educational systems, and the pursuit of knowledge through established channels.

Values and Moral Structures: The Hierophant often represents the moral and ethical structures of society, encouraging individuals to consider their values and how they align with those of their community.

The Hierophant as a Symbol of Consensus: In readings, The Hierophant can indicate a need for consensus or the seeking of advice from established wisdom and recognized authorities.

"The Hierophant" thus serves as a reminder of the value of tradition, mentorship, and cultural wisdom. He encourages exploring and respecting traditional paths, balancing societal norms with personal beliefs, and seeking guidance and wisdom from established sources for greater understanding and spiritual growth.

The Lovers

"The Lovers," typically numbered as the sixth card in the Major Arcana of tarot decks, symbolizes love, harmony, relationships, and significant choices. This card often features two figures, representing a deep connection or partnership, with an angel or Cupid figure above, symbolizing divine influence or fate's role in their bond. The imagery of "The Lovers" emphasizes the concept of duality and choice, where each path leads to distinct outcomes in personal relationships and self-realization.

Psychologically, The Lovers signifies the harmonization of opposing forces within the psyche. It embodies the Jungian concepts of 'anima' and 'animus,' the inner feminine and masculine aspects, suggesting a need for balance and unity within oneself. In readings, The Lovers points to crucial decisions regarding relationships or core values, underscoring the importance of balance and harmony in choices and integrating different aspects of one's personality for personal growth.

The Lovers' presence in a spread indicates a time of critical personal choices, often about intimate relationships, personal beliefs, or core values. This card promotes partnership harmony, urging alignment with actual values and careful consideration in decisions. It emphasizes the significance of relationships in personal development and the impact of choices on one's life path.

When reversed, The Lovers may suggest relationship struggles, imbalance, or misalignment of values, indicating challenges in commitment or decision-making. It can reflect internal conflicts, highlighting the importance of self-awareness and honest communication in resolving personal dilemmas or relationship issues.

Through Carl Jung's lens, The Lovers symbolizes the collective unconscious's aspect of duality and human connection. It represents the psychological journey of integrating various self-aspects to achieve wholeness, often reflected in the choices and relationships that shape our lives.

"The Lovers" stands as a symbol of the power of relationships and choice. It personifies love, harmony, and the union of contrasting elements, advocating thoughtful decision-making and meaningful connections. This card invites a deep exploration of one's desires, values, and the role of relationships in personal evolution.

Relationship Dynamics: The Lovers delves into relationship dynamics, stressing communication, understanding, and compromise in maintaining harmony. It emphasizes the role of empathy and emotional intelligence in navigating the complexities of partnerships.

Integration of the Self: The card suggests integrating various self aspects, including the masculine and feminine energies, for a balanced and harmonious personality. It encourages embracing all facets of one's identity and recognizing the strength in diversity within oneself.

Choices and Consequences: The Lovers accentuates the profound impact of choices on life's journey. It encourages alignment with one's deepest values and beliefs in decision-making, recognizing that each choice shapes the future.

Moral and Ethical Decisions: The card often highlights moral or ethical dilemmas, prompting introspection and adherence to personal ethics. It suggests that moral integrity is crucial in defining one's character and life path.

The Lovers as a Symbol of Unity: In readings, The Lovers can signify the convergence of different elements to create something more significant, symbolizing unity, collaboration, and the power of combining strengths.

Emotional and Spiritual Growth: The Lovers suggests that relationships and choices are vital for emotional and spiritual development, offering rich experiences for learning and self-discovery. It highlights the growth of facing relationship challenges and making difficult choices.

The Lovers in Decision-Making: This card often signals a critical decision-making phase, where choices bear long-term implications, shaping personal life and impacting others.

Harmony in Duality: The Lovers represents finding harmony in contrasting viewpoints or characteristics. It acknowledges the beauty and strength of diversity, encouraging a balanced and inclusive perspective.

"The Lovers" is a powerful reminder of the importance of relationships, the impact of choices, and the pursuit of balance and harmony. It encourages embracing love and connections, making thoughtful decisions, and seeking unity in diversity for personal fulfillment and growth.

Chariot

"The Chariot," typically numbered as the seventh card in the Major Arcana of tarot decks, represents determination, control, and victory. This card usually features a figure riding a chariot, often drawn by two sphinxes or horses, symbolizing opposing forces the charioteer must control. The armored charioteer signifies strength and protection, while the city or kingdom in the background represents the achieved goal or destination.

Psychologically, The Chariot embodies the concept of willpower and the triumph of the mind over emotions. It signifies the individual's ability to focus on their intent and assert control over their environment. In readings, The Chariot suggests overcoming obstacles through determination and self-discipline, highlighting the importance of balance and control in achieving one's goals. It resonates with the Jungian archetype of the 'Hero,' embarking on a journey, facing challenges, and emerging victorious.

The Chariot in a spread indicates a period where assertiveness and confidence are critical. It encourages the querent to take the reins, maintain focus, and steer towards their goals with determination. This card symbolizes the journey towards a goal powered by self-control and ambition.

When reversed, The Chariot may suggest a lack of control or direction, potential aggression, or being pulled in different directions. It might indicate the need to reassess one's path and regain composure and control over one's life.

Through Carl Jung's lens, The Chariot represents the personal journey towards individuation and self-realization. It embodies the psychological struggle of balancing different aspects of the self, harnessing inner strength to overcome external challenges.

"The Chariot" symbolizes the power of determination and control. It personifies the victorious journey, emphasizing the need for self-discipline, focus, and balance in overcoming obstacles. The card suggests that success is attainable through willpower and control.

Dynamic Progress and Movement: The Chariot highlights the importance of progress and forward movement. It suggests an active phase in life, marked by significant achievements and advancements.

Balancing Opposing Forces: The Chariot emphasizes balancing opposing forces within oneself, such as emotions and logic or different aspects of one's personality, to move forward effectively.

Overcoming Challenges: The card is often associated with overcoming challenges and obstacles, demonstrating that perseverance and determination are crucial to success.

Control and Mastery: The Chariot symbolizes control and mastery over one's circumstances. It encourages taking charge of one's life and steering it towards desired outcomes.

Self-Confidence and Assertiveness: The Chariot symbolizes self-confidence and assertiveness, urging the querent to assert themselves and their ambitions confidently.

The Chariot as a Symbol of Victory: In readings, The Chariot often heralds victory and success, especially after a period of struggle or competition.

Harnessing Inner Strength: The card suggests that inner strength and resilience are essential for navigating life's challenges and achieving one's goals.

The Chariot in Career and Ambitions: In career or ambition-related contexts, The Chariot can symbolize a time of rapid advancement, urging a focused, goal-oriented approach.

"The Chariot" is a powerful reminder of the importance of determination, control, and self-discipline in life. It encourages embracing the journey, overcoming obstacles with confidence and focus, and steering towards success and accomplishment with determination and balance.

Strength

"Strength," typically the eighth card in the Major Arcana of tarot decks, represents courage, inner strength, and the mastery of one's instincts. This card often depicts a figure calmly and gently taming a lion, symbolizing the harmonious control of raw power and animalistic impulses. The infinity symbol above the figure's head signifies eternal wisdom and spiritual power, underscoring the card's theme of inner strength and resilience.

Psychologically, Strength embodies the concept of emotional and mental fortitude. It signifies the capacity to face challenges with grace and patience and the ability to channel and transform primal emotions and desires positively. In readings, Strength suggests overcoming obstacles through inner courage and conviction, highlighting the importance of compassion, self-control, and resilience in dealing with difficult situations. It resonates with the Jungian archetype of the 'Heroine' or 'Hero,' facing trials with bravery and a calm demeanor.

The presence of Strength in a spread indicates a time where inner fortitude and a gentle approach are more effective than brute force. It encourages the querent to draw on their inner reserves of strength, to approach challenges with empathy and understanding, and to harness their inner power to overcome adversity.

When reversed, Strength may suggest self-doubt, weakness, or a lack of control over one's instincts. It might indicate a need to cultivate self-confidence, face fears, or learn to manage one's inner forces more effectively.

Through Carl Jung's theories, Strength represents integrating and mastering the shadow self. It embodies the psychological journey of recognizing and transforming one's darker impulses and fears into constructive energies.

"Strength" symbolizes the power of inner resilience and courage. It personifies the triumph of the spirit over external challenges, emphasizing the need for self-awareness, compassion, and inner fortitude in facing life's trials. The card suggests that true strength lies in emotional and mental resilience, not just physical force.

Inner Strength and Emotional Resilience: Strength highlights the importance of inner strength and emotional resilience. It suggests that facing challenges with a calm and compassionate mindset is crucial for personal growth and overcoming difficulties.

Mastering Instincts and Desires: The card emphasizes mastering one's instincts and desires. It encourages understanding and transforming primal emotions and impulses into positive forces.

Gentle Power and Patience: Strength symbolizes the effectiveness of soft power and patience. It advocates for a kind and understanding approach to dealing with challenges, both internally and in interactions with others.

Overcoming Fear and Self-Doubt: The card often signifies overcoming fear and self-doubt. It invites the querent to build self-confidence and courage to face life's uncertainties.

Strength as a Symbol of Courage: In readings, Strength often heralds a period of courage and bravery, especially in the face of adversity or personal trials.

Harnessing Inner Resources: The card suggests that accessing and harnessing one's inner resources is essential for navigating life's challenges and achieving one's goals.

Strength in Personal Relationships: In personal relationships, Strength can symbolize the need for empathy, understanding, and patience in fostering healthy and supportive connections.

Balancing Inner and Outer Strength: The card presents a balanced view of strength, advocating for harmonizing inner emotional strength with outer actions and behaviors.

"Strength" is a powerful reminder of the importance of inner courage, resilience, and the mastery of one's instincts. It encourages embracing inner strength, facing challenges with compassion and patience, and recognizing the power of gentle perseverance in personal development and overcoming life's obstacles.

Hermit

"The Hermit," typically the ninth card in the Major Arcana of tarot decks, symbolizes introspection, wisdom, and guidance. This card often depicts a solitary figure standing in a desolate landscape or atop a mountain, holding a lantern that sheds light in the darkness. The Hermit's cloak represents protection from external distractions, and the lantern symbolizes the inner light of wisdom and knowledge.

Psychologically, The Hermit embodies the journey inward to the depths of the self. It signifies the quest for personal truth, self-awareness, and the understanding that comes from deep reflection. In readings, The Hermit suggests a period of contemplation, solitude, and seeking inner answers, highlighting the importance of withdrawing from the noise of the external world to connect with one's inner wisdom. It resonates with the Jungian archetype of the 'Wise Old Man,' offering guidance, reflection, and deep insight.

The Hermit, in a spread, signals a time for introspection and self-discovery. It encourages the querent to embrace solitude, to reflect deeply on their life journey, and to seek inner guidance. This card symbolizes the need for a personal retreat to gain clarity and understanding.

When reversed, The Hermit may indicate isolation, loneliness, or being overly reflective. It might suggest the need to reconnect with the outside world or to balance solitude with social interaction.

Through Carl Jung's theories, The Hermit represents the inner journey of exploring the unconscious mind. It embodies the psychological process of introspection and the exploration of the deeper aspects of the self, often revealing hidden truths and insights.

"The Hermit" symbolizes the power of introspection and the quest for wisdom. It personifies the search for meaning, emphasizing the need for self-awareness, solitude, and inner guidance in understanding life's mysteries. The card suggests wisdom and guidance often come from within rather than external sources.

Solitude and Inner Journey: The Hermit highlights the value of solitude and the inner journey. It suggests that reflection and introspection are crucial for personal growth and self-understanding.

Seeking Deeper Understanding: The card emphasizes pursuing deeper understanding and truth. It encourages delving into one's subconscious to uncover hidden aspects of the self.

Guidance and Wisdom: The Hermit symbolizes the pursuit of guidance and wisdom. It advocates seeking knowledge and insights, both from within and from wise mentors or guides.

Balance Between Solitude and Society: The card often reflects the balance between solitude and social engagement. It suggests finding harmony between personal introspection and social connections.

Spiritual Quest and Enlightenment: The Hermit is associated with the spiritual quest and the search for enlightenment. It invites the querent to explore their spiritual beliefs and seek deeper spiritual connections.

The Hermit as a Symbol of Reflection: In readings, The Hermit often signals a time for reflection and contemplation, especially when facing significant life decisions or challenges.

Inner Light and Self-Discovery: The card suggests that the journey to self-discovery is illuminated by one's inner light, symbolized by the lantern. It emphasizes the importance of inner wisdom in guiding life's path.

The Hermit in Personal Growth: In the context of personal growth, The Hermit can symbolize a phase of learning and evolving, driven by introspective and reflective practices.

"The Hermit" is a profound reminder of the importance of introspection, solitude, and the search for inner wisdom. It encourages embracing the journey within, seeking deeper understanding and enlightenment, and recognizing the value of solitude and reflection in personal development and growth.

Wheel of Fortune

"The Wheel of Fortune," often numbered as the tenth card in the Major Arcana of tarot decks, represents the cyclical nature of life, change, and destiny. This card typically depicts a giant wheel surrounded by various creatures or figures, symbolizing the constant rotation of life's experiences and fortunes. The wheel often includes symbols or letters that represent the ups and downs of life, emphasizing the theme of fate and the transient nature of success and failure.

Psychologically, The Wheel of Fortune embodies the concept of life's unpredictability and the inevitability of change. It signifies the ever-changing cycles of life and the need to adapt to shifting circumstances. In readings, The Wheel of Fortune suggests a turning point or a significant change in one's life trajectory, underscoring the importance of staying centered and adaptable in uncertainty. It resonates with the Jungian idea of synchronicity, where seemingly random events hold more profound meaning and significance.

The presence of The Wheel of Fortune in a spread signals a phase of transition, where external factors might bring about significant changes. It encourages the querent to embrace the flow of life, to remain open to opportunities, and to understand that every situation is temporary and part of a larger cycle.

When reversed, The Wheel of Fortune may indicate resistance to change, a feeling of being stuck, or a period of bad luck. It might suggest the need to let go of the desire for control and to accept life's natural flow and rhythms.

Through Carl Jung's lens, The Wheel of Fortune represents the collective unconscious's aspect of fate and the interconnectedness of all things. It embodies the idea that life is a series of interconnected cycles and experiences, each with its lessons and opportunities.

"The Wheel of Fortune" symbolizes the dynamic nature of life and the concept of destiny. It personifies the change cycle, emphasizing flexibility, adaptability, and acceptance of life's ups and downs. The card suggests embracing change and understanding life's cyclical nature are essential to personal growth and fulfillment.

Cycles of Life and Change: The Wheel of Fortune highlights the cyclical nature of life, emphasizing that change is constant and inevitable. It suggests that life's experiences, both good and bad, are transient and part of a larger pattern.

Adaptability and Flexibility: The card underscores the importance of adaptability and flexibility. It encourages adjusting one's perspective and approach to life's changing circumstances.

Fate and Destiny: The Wheel of Fortune is associated with fate and destiny. It invites contemplation on the role of fate in life and how one's actions interact with destiny.

Transition and Transformation: The card often signals a period of transition and transformation. It suggests that significant changes can lead to personal growth and new opportunities.

Embracing Uncertainty: The Wheel of Fortune encourages embracing uncertainty and the unknown. It advocates for finding stability within oneself amidst external changes.

The Wheel of Fortune as a Symbol of Opportunity: In readings, The Wheel of Fortune can herald a time of new opportunities and possibilities, especially following a period of stagnation or difficulty.

Letting Go of Control: The card suggests controlling every aspect of life is futile. It emphasizes the value of letting go and trusting in the natural progression of events.

The Wheel of Fortune in Life's Journey: In the context of life's journey, The Wheel of Fortune can symbolize the various phases and experiences that shape one's path, reminding the querent that each phase holds its unique lessons and purpose.

"The Wheel of Fortune" is a powerful reminder of life's ever-changing nature and the constant motion of the wheel of destiny. It encourages embracing change, staying adaptable, and recognizing that each wheel turn brings new challenges and opportunities for growth and evolution.

Justice

"Justice," typically the eleventh card in the Major Arcana of tarot decks, symbolizes fairness, balance, and the law of cause and effect. This card often depicts a figure seated between pillars, like The High Priestess, but with a scale in one hand and a sword in the other. The scale represents balance and fairness, while the sword signifies the power of decision and action. The figure's often blindfolded representation indicates impartiality and the objective nature of justice.

Psychologically, Justice embodies the principle of karma and the importance of decisions and their consequences. It signifies the need for balance in thoughts and actions and the understanding that every action reacts. In readings, Justice suggests a time to weigh decisions carefully, to seek fairness and equilibrium, and to understand the impact of one's actions. It resonates with the Jungian archetype of the 'Judge' or 'Lawgiver,' reflecting the moral and ethical decision-making principles.

The presence of Justice in a spread signals a period of evaluation and judgment, where honesty and integrity are crucial. It encourages the querent to seek truth and fairness in their dealings and to be mindful of the long-term effects of their actions.

When reversed, Justice may suggest injustice, unfairness, or a lack of accountability. It might indicate the need to reevaluate one's sense of fairness or to address situations where justice has not been served.

Through Carl Jung's theories, Justice represents the collective unconscious's aspect of moral reasoning and ethical judgment. It embodies the psychological process of evaluating one's actions and beliefs in light of societal norms and personal ethics.

"Justice" symbolizes the power of fairness and moral principles. It personifies the pursuit of balance and truth, emphasizing the need for ethical conduct, impartiality, and the understanding of actions and consequences. The card suggests fairness and accountability are crucial for personal integrity and social harmony.

Moral and Ethical Decision-Making: Justice highlights the importance of moral and ethical decisions. It urges the querent to consider the moral implications of their choices and actions.

Balance and Fairness: The card emphasizes the need for balance in various aspects of life, including personal relationships, professional dealings, and inner conflicts.

Karma and Consequences: Justice is often associated with karma, suggesting that actions have consequences, and what one puts into the world will return to them.

Legal Matters and Resolution: The card can signal legal matters or disputes coming to a resolution, emphasizing the need for honesty and integrity in these situations.

Objective Judgment: Justice encourages objective and clear-headed judgment, free from emotional bias or personal prejudices.

Accountability and Responsibility: The card underscores the importance of accountability and taking responsibility for one's actions.

The Pursuit of Truth: Justice is associated with the pursuit of truth, both in the external world and within oneself. It invites introspection and alignment with one's true principles.

Balancing Inner and Outer Worlds: Justice represents the equilibrium between inner beliefs and outer actions, advocating consistency and integrity in both realms.

"Justice" is a powerful reminder of the significance of fairness, ethical conduct, and balance. It encourages making decisions with moral integrity, seeking truth and fairness, and understanding the profound impact of our actions on ourselves and the world around us.

The Hanged Man

"The Hanged Man," typically the twelfth card in the Major Arcana of tarot decks, symbolizes surrender, new perspectives, and personal sacrifice. This card often depicts a figure suspended upside-down by one foot, suggesting a state of limbo or contemplation. The serene expression on the figure's face indicates that the suspension and sacrifice are voluntary, and the cross-legged position symbolizes the intersection of the material and spiritual worlds. A halo around the figure's head in many depictions signifies enlightenment or a higher understanding achieved through this experience.

Psychologically, The Hanged Man represents a need to pause and reassess, inviting a shift in perspective. It signifies the importance of letting go of conventional thinking and outdated beliefs to gain insight or enlightenment. In readings, The Hanged Man suggests a period of introspection and waiting, urging the querent to embrace a different viewpoint or to release preconceived notions. This card aligns with the Jungian concept of confronting and integrating the shadow self, where such suspension offers a chance for deep self-reflection and transformation.

The appearance of The Hanged Man in a spread signals a time where stepping back and reassessing is more beneficial than pressing forward. It encourages the querent to embrace patience, to seek wisdom in stillness, and to consider alternate approaches and perspectives.

When reversed, The Hanged Man may indicate resistance to change, stagnation, or unwillingness to view things from a new angle. It might suggest the need to embrace change, relinquish control, and be open to the lessons found in surrender and acceptance.

Through Carl Jung's theories, The Hanged Man represents the journey into the deeper aspects of the unconscious. It embodies the process of self-sacrifice and surrender as paths to uncover hidden truths and self-awareness.

"The Hanged Man" symbolizes the importance of pause, perspective, and personal sacrifice. It personifies the need to let go for greater understanding, emphasizing the virtues of patience, acceptance, and open-mindedness. The card suggests that transformative insights often come from looking at things differently and embracing new perspectives.

Surrender and Letting Go: The Hanged Man highlights the significance of surrendering and letting go of old patterns or beliefs. It suggests that personal growth often requires releasing what no longer serves us.

Gaining New Perspectives: The card emphasizes the value of seeing things differently. It advocates for considering alternative approaches and understanding that new insights can lead to significant personal revelations.

Patience and Waiting: The Hanged Man symbolizes patience and waiting. It advises taking time for introspection and not rushing decisions or actions.

Transformation Through Sacrifice: The card often signifies that personal growth and transformation can result from sacrifice and letting go of one's previous self or beliefs.

Reversal of Perspectives: The Hanged Man can imply a need to reassess one's priorities or values, suggesting a shift in perspective is necessary for personal development.

Spiritual Enlightenment: In readings, The Hanged Man may indicate a phase of spiritual growth or awakening, achieved through reflection and a different understanding of life's challenges.

Inner Peace and Acceptance: The card encourages inner peace by accepting current circumstances and understanding that some situations require yielding control.

The Hanged Man in Personal Development: In the context of personal development, The Hanged Man symbolizes learning and growth that often comes from introspection, acceptance, and viewing life from a new angle.

"The Hanged Man" is a profound reminder of the value of introspection, surrender, and viewing life's challenges from new perspectives. It encourages embracing periods of stillness and contemplation as opportunities for profound personal growth and transformation.

The Death Card

"Death," often the thirteenth card in the Major Arcana of tarot decks, symbolizes profound transformation, the end of a cycle, and the seeds of new beginnings. This card is typically represented by a skeletal figure, the Grim Reaper, signifying the universal nature of change and endings. The figure might be seen riding a horse or standing among people from various societal strata, illustrating that transformation touches all aspects of life. The imagery often includes a rising sun or other symbols of renewal, emphasizing the inevitable cycle of rebirth that follows endings.

Psychologically, Death marks the essential process of letting go and the inevitability of change for personal growth. It embodies the shedding of old ways to make space for new opportunities and perspectives, reflecting life's continual evolution. In readings, the Death card often signals a significant transformation phase, suggesting the closure of one chapter and the start of another. It highlights the need to release past attachments and outdated self-concepts to progress and evolve. This card resonates with the Jungian theme of the death-rebirth archetype, a core aspect of the human psyche's transformative processes.

In a spread, the presence of Death signifies a period of significant transformation. It urges the querent to embrace this period of change, understanding that while such transitions can be challenging, they are necessary for growth and revitalization. This card invites introspection and acceptance of life's transformative cycles, encouraging a positive perspective on change as a catalyst for renewal.

When reversed, the Death card may indicate a resistance to change, a clinging to the familiar, or fear of the unknown. It might suggest the necessity of confronting these fears to move forward, emphasizing the importance of embracing life's natural cycles of transformation and renewal.

Through the lens of Carl Jung's theories, Death represents the deep processes within the unconscious that are involved in letting go, transformation, and renewal. It symbolizes the psychological journey of abandoning the old self and emerging a new, more evolved identity.

"Death" epitomizes the concept of change and the transformative power of endings and new beginnings. It personifies the inevitability and necessity of transitions, emphasizing the importance of acceptance, release, and openness to new possibilities. This card underscores that embracing change and the dissolution of the old is crucial for personal growth, rebirth, and discovering new potential.

The card's focus on transformation and renewal highlights life's dynamic and ever-changing nature. It suggests that endings, often perceived as unfavorable, are essential for personal development and the birth of new ideas and pathways. The transformation process depicted in the Death Card is not only about loss but also about the potential for further growth and opportunities that arise from change.

Letting Go and Embracing Change: The Death Card emphasizes the importance of releasing what is no longer beneficial, encouraging a detachment from past habits, thoughts, or relationships that impede growth.

Cycles of Life and Nature's Rhythms: The card reflects the natural rhythms and cycles in life, where endings and beginnings are intertwined. It speaks to the natural order of life, where every ending is a precursor to a new beginning.

Resilience in the Face of Change: Death encourages resilience and ability in life's changes. It suggests finding strength and growth through transformation challenges, reinforcing that enduring difficult transitions can lead to personal empowerment and enlightenment.

The Metaphor of Rebirth: The Death card often carries the metaphor of rebirth, signifying that with every ending, there is the potential for something new and revitalizing to emerge. It invites the querent to view significant changes as opportunities for renewal and self-discovery.

The Universality of Transformation: The card highlights the universal nature of change and transformation. It suggests that change is an inevitable part of the human experience, touching all aspects of life regardless of one's status or position.

Spiritual and Personal Evolution: In readings, Death can signal a time of profound spiritual and personal evolution. It indicates a phase where the individual is shedding their former self and emerging with a deeper understanding of their true essence and purpose.

Confronting and Accepting Endings: The card encourages facing and accepting the reality of endings. It advocates for acknowledging the impermanence of situations and relationships as a pathway to growth and maturity.

The Death Card in Personal Growth: In the context of personal growth, Death symbolizes the shedding of outdated beliefs, attitudes, or behaviors. It marks a phase of self-transformation and the development of a more authentic self.

"Death" serves as a powerful reminder of life's transformative nature. It encourages embracing change, recognizing the necessity of endings for growth, and viewing life's transitions as opportunities for development and renewal. The card underscores the value of resilience, adaptability, and acceptance in personal and spiritual evolution.

Temperance

"Temperance," typically the fourteenth card in the Major Arcana of tarot decks, symbolizes balance, moderation, and harmony. This card is often depicted as an angelic figure pouring liquid between two cups, signifying the flow and alchemy of life. The angel, standing with one foot in water and one on land, represents the balance between the subconscious and the conscious, the spiritual and the material. The sun rising in the background symbolizes the dawning of understanding and enlightenment from equilibrium.

Psychologically, Temperance embodies the integration of opposites and the achievement of inner harmony. It signifies the need for moderation and self-control in various aspects of life and the importance of adapting to changing circumstances. In readings, Temperance suggests a period of self-evaluation and adjustment, highlighting the need for patience and compromise to achieve balance. It resonates with the Jungian concept of individuation, where the merging of dual aspects leads to a well-rounded and centered self.

The presence of Temperance in a spread indicates a time to seek equilibrium and avoid extremes. It encourages the querent to embrace a balanced approach in life, to harmonize opposing forces, and to find a middle ground in conflicts or dilemmas.

When reversed, Temperance may suggest imbalance, excess, or discord. It might indicate a need to reassess life's priorities, restore balance, and avoid overindulgence or extremes in behavior.

Through Carl Jung's theories, Temperance represents the psychological process of integrating and harmonizing the various aspects of the self. It embodies the idea of creating inner peace and balance through understanding and uniting different elements of one's personality and experiences.

"Temperance" symbolizes the importance of balance, moderation, and the blending of opposites. It personifies the pursuit of middle ground and equilibrium, emphasizing the value of adapting and harmonizing different aspects of life. The card suggests that achieving a state of inner calm and balance is critical to personal growth and fulfillment.

Finding Balance in Life: Temperance emphasizes the importance of finding balance in all areas of life, including personal relationships, work, and inner emotional states. It advocates for a harmonious approach to life's challenges.

Harmonizing Opposites: The card underscores the necessity of bringing together opposing forces, ideas, emotions, or different aspects of one's life to create a sense of harmony and unity.

Moderation and Self-Control: Temperance is often associated with the idea of moderation. It suggests that avoiding extremes and practicing self-control are vital for maintaining equilibrium.

Adaptability and Flexibility: The card encourages adaptability and flexibility, adjusting to changing circumstances to maintain balance.

Healing and Renewal: Temperance can signal a period of healing and renewal, especially after a time of turmoil or imbalance. It indicates a phase of restoring peace and stability.

The Temperance Card as a Symbol of Alchemy: In readings, Temperance often represents the alchemical process of transforming and blending life's experiences to achieve personal growth and understanding.

Inner Peace and Emotional Stability: The card suggests inner peace and emotional stability. It encourages aligning with one's core values and beliefs to cultivate a calm and centered mind.

Temperance in Decision-Making: In decision-making, Temperance can symbolize the need for thoughtful consideration and balance, avoiding hasty or extreme choices.

"Temperance" is a powerful reminder of the value of equilibrium, moderation, and the synthesis of dualities. It encourages embracing a balanced and harmonious approach to life's journey,

recognizing the importance of blending different elements for overall well-being and personal evolution.

Devil

"The Devil," typically the fifteenth card in the Major Arcana of tarot decks, symbolizes bondage, materialism, and the shadow self. This card often depicts a figure resembling the traditional Christian image of the devil, suggesting temptation and the darker aspects of human nature. The figure is usually shown with two figures chained to it, representing the concept of being trapped or controlled by one's base desires or fears. The chains, however, are often loose, suggesting that the bondage is self-imposed and escape is possible.

Psychologically, The Devil represents the aspects of ourselves that we might be reluctant to acknowledge or confront. It signifies the shadow self, comprising repressed desires, fears, and impulses. In readings, The Devil suggests a period of self-reflection to acknowledge and address these darker aspects. It emphasizes the importance of understanding and integrating the shadow self to achieve personal growth. The card resonates with the Jungian concept of facing the shadow, which involves confronting and accepting the less desirable parts of oneself.

The presence of The Devil in a spread indicates a time to examine one's attachments, addictions, or limiting beliefs. It encourages the querent to recognize and release unhealthy patterns, behaviors, or relationships that may hold them back.

When reversed, The Devil may suggest breaking free from restrictions, overcoming addictions, or a newfound awareness of one's negative patterns. It might indicate a rejection of materialistic or superficial values and a movement toward liberation and authenticity.

Through Carl Jung's theories, The Devil represents the confrontation with the unconscious parts of the self that have been ignored, suppressed, or rejected. It embodies the psychological journey of recognizing and integrating these aspects to achieve a more authentic and whole self.

"The Devil" symbolizes the challenges of facing our inner demons and the struggle against material and superficial temptations. It personifies acknowledging our limitations and negative patterns, emphasizing the need for self-awareness, confrontation, and liberation from self-imposed bonds. The card suggests recognizing and understanding our shadow aspects is crucial for personal development and freedom.

Confronting Inner Demons: The Devil highlights the necessity of confronting inner demons, such as harmful habits, addictions, or negative thought patterns, acknowledging their influence, and striving to overcome them.

Materialism and Superficiality: The card emphasizes the pitfalls of materialism and superficiality, suggesting a need to look beyond material desires and focus on more profound, meaningful aspirations.

The Illusion of Bondage: The Devil represents the illusion of bondage and the realization that many of our limitations are self-imposed. It advocates recognizing and releasing these self-created chains.

Empowerment through Awareness: The card encourages empowerment through self-awareness. Understanding our darker nature can lead to personal strength and liberation.

Shadow Self and Integration: The Devil is closely linked with the concept of the shadow self in Jungian psychology. It invites exploration and integration of the shadow to achieve a balanced and authentic self.

Breaking Free from Restriction: In readings, The Devil can signal the process of breaking free from restrictions or limitations, whether self-imposed or external, urging a pursuit of personal freedom and authenticity.

Transformation and Renewal: The card often signifies transformation and renewal, especially after recognizing and addressing the aspects of life that are unfulfilling or harmful.

The Devil in Personal and Spiritual Growth: In the context of personal and spiritual growth, The Devil can symbolize the challenging journey of confronting and transcending one's lower nature, paving the way for a more enlightened and liberated existence.

"The Devil" is a profound reminder of confronting and understanding our darker aspects. It encourages a journey toward personal freedom, advocating for an honest assessment of our limitations and the pursuit of a more authentic and liberated self.

Tower

"The Tower," typically the sixteenth card in the Major Arcana of tarot decks, symbolizes sudden upheaval, disruption, and revelation. This card is often depicted as a tall tower struck by lightning, with figures falling from it, representing the abrupt and often shocking nature of change. The lightning bolt signifies a flash of insight or a sudden disruption that breaks down existing structures, while the crumbling tower represents the dismantling of established beliefs, lifestyles, or perceptions.

Psychologically, The Tower represents the dismantling of ego constructs and false identities. It signifies the often-painful process of being confronted with truths and realities that shatter one's current understanding or way of life. In readings, The Tower suggests a period of significant and sometimes unexpected change, highlighting the need to let go of outdated beliefs or structures. It resonates with the Jungian concept of the 'sudden collapse of the persona,' where a crisis radically reevaluates one's self-concept and perspective.

The appearance of The Tower in a spread signals a time of significant transformation, often experienced as disruptive or challenging. It encourages the querent to embrace the change as an opportunity for growth and liberation from limiting structures or beliefs.

When reversed, The Tower may suggest resistance to change, denial of reality, or fear of upheaval. It might indicate the need to acknowledge and confront impending changes or to dismantle unhelpful structures in one's life proactively.

Through Carl Jung's theories, The Tower represents the confrontation with deep-seated, often unconscious, aspects of the psyche that can no longer be ignored. It embodies the psychological process of radical transformation, usually initiated by crisis or profound realizations.

"The Tower" symbolizes the inevitable nature of transformative change and the destruction of the old to make way for the new. It personifies the experience of upheaval, emphasizing the need for resilience, acceptance, and the willingness to rebuild. The card suggests that while destruction can be painful, it often paves the way for a more authentic and fulfilling life.

Dramatic Change and Upheaval: The Tower emphasizes the impact of dramatic change and upheaval, suggesting that such events while challenging, are necessary for clearing out what is no longer needed.

Breaking Down Illusions: The card highlights breaking down illusions and false structures. It encourages facing the truth, however uncomfortable it may be, to achieve greater authenticity.

Resilience in Times of Crisis: The Tower symbolizes resilience in crisis. It advocates for finding inner strength and adaptability during times of turmoil.

Revelation and Awakening: The card often signifies revelation and awakening, marking a period where one's consciousness is expanded through unexpected events or insights.

Letting Go of the Past: The Tower suggests letting go of past constructs and beliefs. It invites the querent to release old patterns and embrace the rebuilding process.

The Tower as a Catalyst for Change: In readings, The Tower can signal a powerful catalyst for change, urging the querent to prepare for and adapt to significant shifts in their life.

Opportunities for Rebuilding: The card implies that the destruction of the old creates space for something new and better. It highlights the opportunities that arise from the ashes of the old.

The Tower in Personal Transformation: In the context of personal transformation, The Tower symbolizes the sometimes painful but necessary process of dismantling the ego and false identities, leading to a more authentic and liberated self.

"The Tower" is a stark reminder of life's unpredictability and the transformative power of upheaval. It encourages embracing change as an integral part of growth, recognizing the potential for renewal and redefinition from abandoning outdated structures and beliefs.

Star

"The Star," typically the seventeenth card in the Major Arcana of tarot decks, symbolizes hope, inspiration, and spiritual guidance. This card is often depicted with a serene figure, either kneeling or pouring water, with several stars in the background, including one large, bright star. Running water signifies healing, renewal, and the free flow of emotion and creativity. The stars symbolize hope, guidance, and the soul's light, illuminating the path ahead.

Psychologically, The Star represents a sense of optimism, clarity, and renewed purpose. It signifies the calming of the mind and the rejuvenation of the spirit after a period of turmoil, as seen in The Tower. In readings, The Star suggests a period of tranquility, hope, and positive prospects. It encourages the querent to trust their intuition and to follow the guiding light of their inner wisdom. The card resonates with the Jungian concept of alignment with the Self, where one finds harmony between their conscious and unconscious mind, leading to a sense of wholeness and peace.

The presence of The Star in a spread signals a time of serenity and clarity, where one can see their circumstances with newfound hope and optimism. It encourages the querent to focus on healing and to have faith in the future, understanding that the universe is guiding them.

When reversed, The Star may suggest a loss of hope, disillusionment, or a disconnection from one's inner guidance. It might indicate the need to rediscover faith in oneself and the journey, to realign with one's spiritual path, or to find the light amid darkness.

Through Carl Jung's theories, The Star represents the process of individuation and the realization of the deeper self. It embodies the journey toward self-discovery and the alignment with one's true purpose and potential.

"The Star" symbolizes the light of hope, spiritual clarity, and inspiration. It personifies the sense of guidance and the promise of better times, emphasizing the importance of trust in the process of life and the pursuit of one's true path. The card suggests that maintaining a sense of hope and staying true to oneself are vital for personal fulfillment and spiritual enlightenment.

Renewal and Spiritual Clarity: The Star highlights the theme of renewal and spiritual clarity. It suggests a time of healing and inner peace, where one can clearly understand their path and purpose.

Hope and Optimism: The card embodies the essence of hope and optimism. It encourages looking forward with positivity and embracing a brighter future.

Guidance and Inspiration: The Star symbolizes the role of guidance and inspiration in one's life. It invites the querent to be open to spiritual and creative inspiration, which can illuminate their journey.

Inner Peace and Serenity: The card suggests a period of inner peace and serenity. It encourages finding tranquility within oneself and harmonizing with the natural flow of life.

Trust in the Universe: The Star advocates for trust in the universe and its guidance. It implies that even in darkness, a guiding light is leading the way.

The Star as a Symbol of Healing: In readings, The Star often represents emotional and spiritual healing, indicating a time of rejuvenation and growth.

Rediscovery of Faith and Purpose: The card can signal a rediscovery of faith in oneself and one's purpose, especially after a period of doubt or confusion.

The Star in Personal Development: In the context of personal development, The Star symbolizes the journey towards understanding one's true potential and aligning with one's higher self.

"The Star" is a powerful reminder of the enduring presence of hope and guidance in life. It encourages embracing a period of healing and renewal, maintaining optimism, and following the guiding light of one's inner wisdom and intuition for spiritual growth and self-realization.

Moon

"The Moon," often the eighteenth card in the Major Arcana of tarot decks, symbolizes the subconscious, intuition, and the uncovering of hidden truths. This card typically depicts a night scene featuring a moon with a face, reflecting the dual nature of light and shadow. The imagery often includes a path leading off into the distance, a dog and a wolf, representing the tame and wild aspects of our nature, and a crayfish emerging from the water, symbolizing the depths of the subconscious.

Psychologically, The Moon represents the journey into the deeper, often hidden, layers of the self. It signifies exploring the subconscious mind, where dreams, fears, and repressed emotions reside. In readings, The Moon suggests a time of uncertainty and confusion, encouraging the querent to trust their intuition and to explore their inner depths for clarity. It resonates with the Jungian concept of exploring the shadow self, acknowledging and integrating the less recognized parts of one's psyche.

The presence of The Moon in a spread signals a period of introspection and examination of the subconscious. It encourages the querent to face their fears, to delve into the unknown aspects of their psyche, and to be attentive to dreams and intuitions.

When reversed, The Moon may suggest illusion, deception, or a refusal to delve deeper into one's subconscious. It might indicate the need to distinguish between reality and illusion and to confront hidden truths or fears.

Through Carl Jung's theories, The Moon represents the confrontation with the unconscious, revealing what is hidden, repressed, or unacknowledged. It embodies the psychological journey of illuminating the mind's dark corners and understanding the deeper motivations and fears.

"The Moon" symbolizes the mysteries of the subconscious and the importance of intuition. It personifies the exploration of the unknown and the shadow self, emphasizing the need for introspection and awareness of the less visible aspects of life. The card suggests that navigating through uncertainty and embracing the journey of self-discovery are crucial for personal growth and understanding.

Exploration of the Subconscious: The Moon highlights the exploration of the subconscious mind, inviting the querent to delve into their inner depths to uncover hidden truths and meanings.

Intuition and Inner Guidance: The card emphasizes the importance of intuition and inner guidance. It suggests relying on one's intuitive feelings to navigate through uncertain times.

Facing Hidden Fears: The Moon is often associated with facing hidden fears and anxieties. It encourages acknowledging and confronting these fears to overcome them.

Illusion and Reality: The card invites a careful examination of what may be illusion or deception in one's life, urging a discernment between truth and fantasy.

Dreams and Symbols: The Moon can indicate a time when dreams and symbols are particularly significant, offering insights into the subconscious and emotional state.

The Moon as a Symbol of Reflection: In readings, The Moon often reflects a period of self-reflection, introspection, and seeking answers within.

Emotional Flux and Mood Swings: The card can represent dynamic flux and mood swings, suggesting a need for stability amidst emotional turbulence.

The Moon in Personal Transformation: In the context of personal transformation, The Moon symbolizes the journey through the dark to reach a deeper understanding and enlightenment.

"The Moon" is a profound reminder of the complexities of the subconscious mind and the power of intuition. It encourages embracing the journey into the unknown, acknowledging hidden aspects of the self, and relying on inner wisdom to guide through periods of uncertainty and confusion.

Sun

"The Sun," typically the nineteenth card in the Major Arcana of tarot decks, symbolizes joy, success, and clarity. This card often depicts a radiant sun shining in the sky, illuminating everything around it, and sometimes includes a child or children playing joyfully under its rays. These elements represent the purity, vitality, and openness of enlightenment and understanding. The sun is a universal symbol of life and energy, embodying positivity and warmth.

Psychologically, The Sun represents the awakening to truth and the illumination of what was once hidden. It signifies clarity of thought, optimism, and the conscious mind's most enlightened state. In readings, The Sun suggests a period of happiness and fulfillment where things are clear and success is within reach. It resonates with the Jungian concept of achieving wholeness through integrating all aspects of the self and realizing one's full potential.

The presence of The Sun in a spread signals a time of positivity and achievement. It encourages the querent to embrace joy and success, to express themselves fully, and to celebrate their accomplishments. The Sun conveys vitality and promotes pursuing one's true path confidently and clearly.

When reversed, The Sun may suggest temporary setbacks, a lack of clarity, or diminished joy. It might indicate the need to rediscover one's inner light, to find joy in the simple things, and to remain hopeful despite challenges.

Through Carl Jung's theories, The Sun represents the conscious mind in harmony with the unconscious, symbolizing an integrated and balanced psyche. It embodies the psychological journey of self-realization, where one embraces one's identity with clarity and joy.

"The Sun" symbolizes the radiance of self-awareness and the warmth of success. It personifies the joy of living, the clarity of purpose, and the fulfillment of achieving one's goals. The card suggests that embracing one's true self and celebrating life's blessings are crucial to experiencing profound joy and satisfaction.

Celebration of Life and Vitality: The Sun highlights the celebration of life, vitality, and success. It suggests embracing the joys of life and expressing gratitude for the blessings.

Clarity and Enlightenment: The card emphasizes clarity of thought and enlightenment. It encourages seeking truth and understanding, illuminating the path forward.

Optimism and Positivity: The Sun is often associated with optimism and a positive outlook. It invites maintaining a sunny disposition and expecting good things to happen.

Success and Achievement: The card symbolizes success and achievement. It suggests a period of accomplishment and the fruition of efforts.

Joyful Expression and Creativity: The Sun encourages positive expression and creativity. It invites celebrating one's unique talents and sharing them with the world.

The Sun as a Symbol of Inner Harmony: In readings, The Sun often represents inner harmony and balance. It signifies a state of being where one is at peace with themselves and their surroundings.

Renewal and New Beginnings: The card can signal a time of renewal and new beginnings, infused with energy and enthusiasm for what lies ahead.

The Sun in Personal Growth: In the context of personal growth, The Sun symbolizes the journey toward self-realization and discovering one's true potential and purpose.

"The Sun" is a powerful reminder of the joy and fulfillment of embracing life with positivity and clarity. It encourages celebrating successes, seeking enlightenment, and radiating warmth and vitality, leading to a fulfilling and enriched life experience.

Judgment

"Judgment," typically the twentieth card in the Major Arcana of tarot decks, symbolizes rebirth, inner calling, and reflection. This card is often depicted with an angel, usually Gabriel, blowing a trumpet, with people rising from graves below, signifying awakening and resurrection. This imagery represents a call to a new level of consciousness, a moment of reckoning and self-evaluation, where past actions and decisions are assessed.

Psychologically, Judgment represents a time of self-realization and a deep understanding of one's life journey. It signifies evaluating past experiences and understanding their deeper meanings and implications. In readings, Judgment suggests a period of reflection and self-assessment, urging the querent to heed their inner call and to embrace transformation. It resonates with the Jungian concept of individuation, where one becomes aware of their deeper self and moves towards realizing their true potential.

The presence of Judgment in a spread signals a time for critical evaluation and decision-making. It encourages the querent to take stock of their life, to listen to their inner voice, and to prepare for a significant change or transformation.

When reversed, Judgment may suggest self-doubt, indecision, or ignoring a critical calling. It might indicate the need to reevaluate one's choices, to face unresolved issues, or to heed a neglected inner voice.

Through Carl Jung's theories, Judgment represents the integration of various life experiences, leading to a cohesive sense of self. It embodies the psychological process of synthesizing past experiences and revelations into a unified understanding of one's identity and purpose.

"Judgment" symbolizes the transformative power of self-reflection and the call to a higher understanding. It personifies the awakening to a new level of awareness, emphasizing the need for introspection, self-evaluation, and heeding one's inner call. The card suggests that embracing one's true calling and understanding life's lessons are crucial for personal growth and fulfillment.

Self-Realization and Awakening: Judgment underscores the themes of self-realization and spiritual awakening. It invites the querent to recognize their true potential and to awaken to a higher level of consciousness.

Evaluation and Reflection: The card emphasizes evaluating one's past actions and decisions. It suggests taking time for introspection and understanding the impact of one's choices.

Heeding the Inner Call: Judgment is often associated with responding to one's inner calling or purpose. It encourages listening to one's inner voice and aligning with one's true path.

Transformation and Renewal: The card signifies a period of transformation and renewal, marking a shift from the old self to a new, more enlightened identity.

Embracing Change: Judgment encourages embracing change and the opportunities it brings. It suggests that significant transformations can lead to positive growth and renewal.

The Judgment Card as a Symbol of Reckoning: In readings, Judgment often represents a moment of reckoning or a critical point of decision, urging the querent to make thoughtful choices about their future.

Integration of Experiences: The card highlights the integration of life experiences into a cohesive understanding of oneself, recognizing the lessons and growth that come from past events.

Judgment in Personal Development: In the context of personal development, Judgment symbolizes the journey towards self-awareness and the realization of one's life purpose and potential.

"Judgment" serves as a profound reminder of the importance of introspection, self-awareness, and responding to one's inner calling. It encourages a thorough evaluation of one's life journey, understanding the lessons of the past, and embracing the transformative process of awakening to a more authentic and fulfilling existence.

World

"The World," typically the twenty-first and final card in the Major Arcana of tarot decks, symbolizes completion, achievement, and unity. This card is often depicted with a figure dancing within a laurel wreath, surrounded by the four elements or living beings symbolizing earth, air, fire, and water. This imagery represents the successful conclusion of a journey, the harmony of all elements, and the celebratory nature of accomplishment. The wreath signifies victory and the unending cycle of life, as it forms an ouroboros, a snake eating its tail, symbolizing wholeness and infinity.

Psychologically, The World represents the fulfillment and integration of all aspects of the self. It signifies the achievement of goals, the realization of dreams, and the attainment of a higher state of consciousness. In readings, The World suggests a period of completion and celebration, where one's efforts have come to fruition. It resonates with the Jungian concept of individuation, where the individual achieves a sense of completeness and unity within themselves, harmonizing their conscious and unconscious mind.

The presence of The World in a spread signals a time of accomplishment and satisfaction. It encourages the querent to recognize and celebrate their achievements, to enjoy the sense of wholeness, and to embrace the unity of their experiences.

When reversed, The World may suggest unfinished business, a lack of closure, or a need to integrate certain aspects of one's life. It might indicate the need for further growth or the continuation of the journey to achieve true fulfillment.

Through Carl Jung's theories, The World represents the culmination of the journey towards self-discovery and understanding. It embodies the realization of the true self, the integration of life's lessons, and the achievement of harmony within one's psyche.

"The World" symbolizes the joy of achievement and the completeness of being. It personifies the successful culmination of a journey, emphasizing the importance of acknowledging and celebrating one's accomplishments. The card suggests that reaching a state of wholeness and fulfillment is a significant milestone in one's life journey.

Completion and Fulfillment: The World highlights the theme of completion and fulfillment. It suggests reaching the end of a significant phase or journey, with a sense of accomplishment and satisfaction.

Integration of Experiences: The card emphasizes the integration of diverse experiences, symbolizing the harmony and balance achieved through this process.

Celebration of Success: The World encourages celebrating successes and achievements, recognizing the effort and journey that led to this point.

Sense of Wholeness: The card represents a sense of wholeness and unity, suggesting a balanced and integrated state of being.

Global Awareness and Connection: The World can signify a broadening of perspective, indicating an awareness of one's place in the larger scheme of things and a connection to the world at large.

The World as a Symbol of Enlightenment: In readings, The World often represents enlightenment or a high level of consciousness, signifying a deep understanding of life's mysteries.

Continuation of Growth: When reversed, The World may suggest that the journey is not yet complete, indicating the need for ongoing growth and development.

The World in Personal Development: In the context of personal development, The World symbolizes reaching a significant milestone or level of maturity, where one's experiences have led to a profound understanding of self and life.

"The World" serves as a powerful reminder of the joy and fulfillment that come with achieving one's goals and realizing one's potential. It encourages celebrating life's victories, embracing the completeness of one's journey, and recognizing the interconnectedness of all experiences in the tapestry of life.

The Cups Series

Ace of Cups

"The Ace of Cups," a card in the Minor Arcana of tarot decks, symbolizes emotional beginnings, love, intuition, and creativity. This card typically features a cup or chalice overflowing with water, representing the abundance of emotions and the awakening of feelings. Often, a hand is shown presenting the cup, suggesting that these emotions are being offered or are emerging from the subconscious. The water flowing from the cup symbolizes the free flow of feelings, intuition, and artistic expression.

Psychologically, The Ace of Cups signifies the blossoming of emotions and the opening of the heart. It represents new emotional experiences, such as the beginnings of love, the deepening of emotional understanding, or the onset of a creative or spiritual journey. In readings, The Ace of Cups suggests embracing new emotions and connections, highlighting the importance of intuition and emotional receptiveness in guiding personal interactions and creative endeavors. This card resonates with the Jungian concept of tapping into the collective unconscious, where emotions and creativity originate.

The appearance of The Ace of Cups in a spread signals a period ripe for emotional growth and the exploration of feelings. It encourages the querent to open their heart, to embrace compassion and empathy, and to be receptive to new emotional experiences.

When reversed, The Ace of Cups may suggest emotional repression, blocked intuition, or a reluctance to embrace new feelings. It might indicate the need to address suppressed emotions or to open oneself up to emotional healing and expression.

Through Carl Jung's theories, The Ace of Cups represents the emergence of emotions and intuition from the depths of the unconscious. It embodies the process of emotional awakening and the acknowledgment of one's deeper emotional capacity and creative potential.

"The Ace of Cups" symbolizes the genesis of emotional and intuitive experiences. It personifies new beginnings in the realm of feelings and creativity, emphasizing the need for emotional openness and the embracing of intuitive guidance. The card suggests that genuine emotional expression and creativity are essential for personal fulfillment and growth.

Emotional Openness and Receptivity: The Ace of Cups highlights the importance of being emotionally open and receptive. It suggests that welcoming new feelings and experiences is key to personal development and emotional well-being.

Creative Inspiration: The card signifies a surge of creative inspiration, urging the querent to engage in artistic or imaginative endeavors fueled by their emotional depth and intuition.

Spiritual and Emotional Awakening: The Ace of Cups is often associated with a spiritual or emotional awakening. It invites the exploration of spiritual dimensions and a deeper understanding of one's emotional landscape.

Healing and Emotional Clarity: The card can signal a time for emotional healing and gaining clarity about one's feelings. It encourages addressing emotional wounds to foster emotional well-being.

The Ace of Cups as a Symbol of Love: In readings, The Ace of Cups can indicate the beginning of a new, heartfelt relationship or the deepening of existing emotional bonds.

Nurturing Emotional Relationships: The card emphasizes nurturing emotional relationships, advocating for empathy, understanding, and genuine emotional connection.

Inner Harmony and Peace: The Ace of Cups suggests finding inner harmony and peace. It encourages aligning with one's emotional core and cultivating inner serenity.

The Ace of Cups in Personal Growth: In personal growth contexts, The Ace of Cups can symbolize the emergence of new emotional understanding and the importance of embracing and expressing one's true feelings.

"The Ace of Cups" serves as a profound reminder of the richness of emotional experiences and the power of intuition and creativity. It encourages embracing new emotional journeys, trusting in the flow of feelings, and recognizing the transformative power of love and creativity in personal evolution.

Two of Cups

"The Two of Cups," a card in the Minor Arcana of tarot decks, symbolizes partnership, unity, and emotional connection. This card typically features two individuals exchanging cups, signifying the sharing of emotions and the mutual understanding between people. Often, a caduceus or a winged lion is depicted above the cups, representing healing, balance, and a protective aspect to the relationship. The Two of Cups is about the harmony and attraction found in partnerships, whether romantic, platonic, or professional.

Psychologically, The Two of Cups represents the formation of meaningful relationships and the recognition of emotional bonds. It signifies the mutual respect, attraction, and understanding that form the foundation of strong partnerships. In readings, The Two of Cups suggests a coming together of two forces, emphasizing cooperation, negotiation, and emotional support. It resonates with the Jungian concept of the anima and animus, the inner feminine and masculine energies, and their interplay in forming balanced relationships.

The presence of The Two of Cups in a spread signals a time of forming or deepening connections. It encourages the querent to embrace mutual understanding, to foster emotional support, and to appreciate the value of partnerships in their life.

When reversed, The Two of Cups may suggest disharmony, miscommunication, or imbalance in a relationship. It might indicate the need to address conflicts, to reassess the emotional dynamics, or to restore balance and understanding between parties.

Through Carl Jung's theories, The Two of Cups represents the integration and harmony of dual aspects within oneself or in a relationship. It embodies the psychological process of recognizing and valuing the complementary qualities in oneself and others.

"The Two of Cups" symbolizes the beauty of connection and partnership. It personifies mutual respect, emotional exchange, and the forming of meaningful bonds. The card suggests that building cooperative and harmonious relationships is key to emotional fulfillment and personal growth.

Formation of Bonds and Partnerships: The Two of Cups highlights the importance of forming emotional bonds and partnerships. It suggests that these relationships bring balance and enrichment to one's life.

Mutual Respect and Understanding: The card emphasizes mutual respect and understanding as foundational elements of strong relationships. It encourages open communication and emotional support.

Cooperation and Harmony: The Two of Cups is often associated with cooperation and harmony. It invites working together towards common goals and nurturing mutually beneficial relationships.

Balancing Emotional Needs: The card suggests the importance of balancing emotional needs in a relationship, advocating for empathy and consideration of each other's feelings.

The Two of Cups as a Symbol of Unity: In readings, The Two of Cups often represents unity and the coming together of complementary forces, whether in love, friendship, or business.

Emotional Exchange and Support: The card underscores the value of emotional exchange and support in relationships. It encourages sharing feelings and offering emotional support to strengthen bonds.

Reconciliation and Healing: When reversed, The Two of Cups can indicate the potential for reconciliation and healing in strained relationships, suggesting a need to address and resolve underlying issues.

The Two of Cups in Personal Development: In the context of personal development, The Two of Cups can symbolize the journey of understanding and integrating different aspects of oneself or learning from others to achieve a balanced and harmonious self.

"The Two of Cups" serves as a powerful reminder of the significance of emotional connections and partnerships. It encourages embracing relationships with empathy and respect, recognizing the strength found in unity, and the growth that comes from emotional exchange and mutual support.

Three of Cups

"The Three of Cups," a card in the Minor Arcana of tarot decks, symbolizes celebration, friendship, and community. This card typically depicts three individuals, often shown raising cups in a toast, signifying shared joy, success, and a sense of communal accomplishment. The atmosphere in this card is one of festivity and harmony, reflecting strong social bonds and the joy of coming together with others. The card embodies the spirit of collaboration, mutual support, and the happiness found in social interactions.

Psychologically, The Three of Cups represents the fulfillment and satisfaction derived from shared experiences and communal achievements. It signifies the importance of social bonds and the emotional nourishment that comes from being part of a community. In readings, The Three of Cups suggests a time of joyous gathering, urging the querent to celebrate life's successes with those around them and to foster a sense of community. It resonates with the Jungian concept of the collective unconscious, where shared experiences and cultural celebrations play a crucial role in the human psyche.

The presence of The Three of Cups in a spread signals a period of social harmony and celebration. It encourages the querent to engage in communal activities, to nurture their relationships, and to enjoy the company of friends and family.

When reversed, The Three of Cups may suggest overindulgence, gossip, or discord within a group. It might indicate the need to reassess one's social circle, to address conflicts within a community, or to find a balance between social life and other responsibilities.

Through Carl Jung's theories, The Three of Cups represents the connection with others through shared emotions and experiences. It embodies the psychological benefits of social interaction and the importance of being part of a group or community.

"The Three of Cups" symbolizes the joy and fulfillment found in communal bonds. It personifies the celebration of friendships and shared achievements, emphasizing the need for social interaction and mutual support. The card suggests that embracing community and participating in shared experiences are integral to emotional well-being and happiness.

Celebration and Joy: The Three of Cups highlights the importance of celebration and joy, especially in the context of group achievements or milestones. It suggests taking time to acknowledge and enjoy successes together.

Social Connections and Community: The card emphasizes the value of social connections and being part of a community. It encourages building strong relationships and engaging in communal activities.

Friendship and Support: The Three of Cups is often associated with friendship and mutual support. It invites cherishing and nurturing friendships, recognizing their role in one's life.

Shared Experiences and Collaboration: The card underscores the benefits of shared experiences and collaboration. It suggests that working together with others can lead to collective success and fulfillment.

The Three of Cups as a Symbol of Harmony: In readings, The Three of Cups often represents social harmony and the positive aspects of being part of a group or community.

Balancing Social Life: When reversed, The Three of Cups can indicate the need to balance one's social life with other areas, or it may highlight issues within social groups that need attention.

The Three of Cups in Personal Growth: In the context of personal growth, The Three of Cups can symbolize the journey of finding one's place within a community and the growth that comes from interacting with diverse groups of people.

"The Three of Cups" serves as a powerful reminder of the joy and enrichment that come from social bonds and communal celebrations. It encourages embracing the companionship of friends and family, participating in shared experiences, and recognizing the strength and support found in community connections.

Four of Cups

"The Four of Cups," a card in the Minor Arcana of tarot decks, symbolizes contemplation, apathy, and reevaluation. This card typically depicts a figure sitting under a tree, arms crossed, looking contemplatively at three cups set before them, while a fourth cup is being offered by a hand emerging from a cloud. This imagery represents moments of introspection, where one might feel disenchanted or disinterested in what is currently being offered, reflecting a period of inner reflection or emotional withdrawal.

Psychologically, The Four of Cups signifies a time of inward focus, where the individual may be reassessing their desires, feelings, and emotional satisfactions. It represents a state of contemplation, where one might be considering what truly brings them fulfillment and joy. In readings, The Four of Cups suggests a need to pause and reflect, to reassess one's situation, and to consider whether current opportunities align with one's true desires. This card resonates with the Jungian concept of the inner journey, where introspection leads to a deeper understanding of the self and reevaluation of one's goals and motivations.

The appearance of The Four of Cups in a spread signals a period of introspection and potential dissatisfaction. It encourages the querent to examine their emotional state and to be mindful of opportunities that may be overlooked due to a preoccupied or disenchanted mindset.

When reversed, The Four of Cups may suggest emerging from a period of introspection, regaining interest, or a renewed appreciation for life's offerings. It might indicate the recognition of missed opportunities or the need to become more engaged with the external world.

Through Carl Jung's theories, The Four of Cups represents the process of turning inward to explore one's true feelings and desires. It embodies the psychological journey of understanding one's emotional landscape and reassessing what brings true satisfaction and happiness.

"The Four of Cups" symbolizes the importance of introspection and emotional reevaluation. It personifies a contemplative state, emphasizing the need for self-reflection and careful consideration of one's emotional needs and desires. The card suggests that periods of introspection are necessary for personal growth and emotional clarity.

Introspection and Self-Reflection: The Four of Cups highlights the significance of introspection and self-reflection. It suggests taking time to consider one's emotional needs and whether they are being met.

Reevaluation of Desires: The card emphasizes the reevaluation of one's desires and satisfactions. It encourages questioning what truly brings fulfillment and reassessing life's goals.

Apathy and Discontent: The Four of Cups is often associated with feelings of apathy and discontent. It invites addressing the root causes of these feelings and considering ways to regain emotional engagement.

Mindfulness of Opportunities: The card suggests being mindful of opportunities that may be overlooked during periods of introspection or dissatisfaction.

The Four of Cups as a Symbol of Contemplation: In readings, The Four of Cups often represents a contemplative phase, where the querent is encouraged to pause and reflect on their current emotional state and life direction.

Emerging from Introspection: When reversed, The Four of Cups can indicate emerging from a period of introspection, ready to reengage with the world and appreciate new opportunities.

The Four of Cups in Personal Growth: In the context of personal growth, The Four of Cups symbolizes the journey of understanding one's true emotional needs and desires, leading to a more authentic and satisfying life.

"The Four of Cups" serves as a powerful reminder of the value of introspection and the reevaluation of one's emotional landscape. It encourages taking a step back to reflect on personal fulfillment, to become more aware of potential opportunities, and to align more closely with one's true desires and needs.

Five of Cups

"The Five of Cups," a card in the Minor Arcana of tarot decks, symbolizes loss, regret, and focusing on the negative. This card typically features a figure cloaked in sorrow, looking down at three spilled cups, representing a sense of grief or disappointment over what has been lost. Behind the figure, two cups still stand upright, suggesting that not all is lost and that opportunities for emotional replenishment and recovery remain.

Psychologically, The Five of Cups represents the process of dealing with emotional pain and the challenge of overcoming a pessimistic outlook. It signifies the natural human tendency to lament what is gone while often overlooking the potential and possibilities that still exist. In readings, The Five of Cups suggests a period of mourning or sadness, encouraging the querent to acknowledge their feelings of loss but also to recognize the value and hope in what remains. This card resonates with the Jungian concept of confronting and working through emotional pain as a necessary step towards healing and growth.

The presence of The Five of Cups in a spread signals a time to address feelings of sorrow or regret. It encourages the querent to process their emotions, to learn from their experiences, and to eventually turn their attention to the positive aspects that are still present in their life.

When reversed, The Five of Cups may suggest the beginning of emotional recovery, moving past regret, or a shift in focus from what has been lost to what can still be gained. It might indicate finding closure, healing from past hurts, or learning to appreciate the positive aspects of one's life.

Through Carl Jung's theories, The Five of Cups represents the emotional journey through loss and the eventual reintegration of the self. It embodies the psychological process of acknowledging pain, learning from it, and finding a way to move forward with a renewed perspective.

"The Five of Cups" symbolizes the complexities of emotional loss and the challenge of overcoming a focus on the negative. It personifies the experience of grief and disappointment, emphasizing the importance of acknowledging and processing these emotions. The card suggests that while acknowledging loss is crucial, it is equally important to recognize and embrace the opportunities and positives that remain.

Dealing with Emotional Pain: The Five of Cups highlights the significance of dealing with emotional pain and loss. It suggests the importance of allowing oneself to grieve while also maintaining an awareness of ongoing life.

Acknowledging Loss and Regret: The card emphasizes the natural response of acknowledging loss and regret. It encourages facing these emotions and understanding their impact.

Looking Beyond Disappointment: The Five of Cups is often associated with the challenge of looking beyond disappointment. It invites finding strength in adversity and focusing on the potential for positive change.

Hope Amidst Sorrow: The card suggests that even in sorrow, there is hope. It encourages focusing on the positive aspects that remain and the potential for emotional healing.

The Five of Cups as a Symbol of Reflection: In readings, The Five of Cups often represents a reflective phase, where the querent is prompted to consider their losses and the lessons they bring.

Moving Past Grief: When reversed, The Five of Cups can indicate moving past grief and starting to focus more on the positives that life has to offer.

The Five of Cups in Personal Growth: In the context of personal growth, The Five of Cups symbolizes the journey through emotional challenges and the learning that comes from experiencing and overcoming sadness and disappointment.

"The Five of Cups" serves as a profound reminder of the dual nature of emotional experiences. It encourages embracing the full spectrum of emotions, from grief to hope, recognizing that each experience contributes to personal depth, resilience, and a more nuanced understanding of life's complexities.

Six of Cups

"The Six of Cups," a card in the Minor Arcana of tarot decks, symbolizes nostalgia, fond memories, and revisiting the past. This card typically features figures, often children, sharing cups filled with flowers, representing the innocence and joy of childhood and the comfort of familiar, pleasant memories. The serene and gentle atmosphere in the imagery suggests a return to simpler, happier times and the positive aspects of revisiting one's past.

Psychologically, The Six of Cups represents the emotional connection to the past and the impact of memories on the present. It signifies a longing for the simplicity and purity of earlier times and the comfort found in reminiscence. In readings, The Six of Cups suggests a period of reflection on past experiences, encouraging the querent to draw upon positive memories and experiences for guidance or solace. This card resonates with the Jungian concept of the collective unconscious, where shared human experiences and archetypes from the past influence current emotional states.

The presence of The Six of Cups in a spread signals a time to embrace nostalgia and the lessons from the past. It encourages the querent to reconnect with their inner child, to find joy in simple pleasures, and to appreciate the formative experiences that have shaped them.

When reversed, The Six of Cups may suggest being overly anchored in the past, an inability to move forward, or idealizing the past at the expense of the present. It might indicate the need to balance nostalgia with the demands of the current reality and to integrate past experiences into a healthy perspective for growth.

Through Carl Jung's theories, The Six of Cups represents the exploration of the past and its influence on the individual's psyche. It embodies the psychological process of understanding how past experiences and memories contribute to one's current emotional landscape.

"The Six of Cups" symbolizes the warmth and comfort of memories and the influence of the past on the present. It personifies the reflective journey into one's history, emphasizing the value of nostalgia and the impact of childhood experiences. The card suggests that revisiting and cherishing past moments can provide emotional depth and insight into current life situations.

Nostalgia and the Comfort of Memories: The Six of Cups highlights the significance of nostalgia and the comfort found in revisiting fond memories. It suggests that reflecting on the past can provide solace and joy.

Reconnecting with the Inner Child: The card emphasizes the importance of reconnecting with one's inner child. It encourages embracing the innocence, playfulness, and simplicity of childhood.

Lessons from the Past: The Six of Cups is often associated with the lessons and experiences from the past. It invites integrating these lessons into the present to enrich one's life.

Cherishing Simplicity: The card suggests finding joy in simple pleasures and the small moments that bring happiness, reminiscent of childhood experiences.

The Six of Cups as a Symbol of Innocence: In readings, The Six of Cups often represents a return to innocence and the pure, unburdened emotions associated with childhood.

Balancing Past and Present: When reversed, The Six of Cups can indicate the need to balance nostalgia with current responsibilities, ensuring that memories enhance rather than hinder present-day life.

The Six of Cups in Personal Growth: In the context of personal growth, The Six of Cups symbolizes the journey of exploring one's past and understanding its impact on their emotional well-being and development.

"The Six of Cups" serves as a powerful reminder of the enduring influence of the past and the richness of memories. It encourages embracing nostalgia, reconnecting with one's roots, and appreciating the formative experiences that shape our emotional world, offering a deeper understanding of oneself and a renewed sense of joy and simplicity.

Seven of Cups

"The Seven of Cups," a card in the Minor Arcana of tarot decks, symbolizes choices, illusions, and imagination. This card is often depicted with a figure gazing at seven cups filled with various symbols, representing different dreams, opportunities, and choices, some realistic and others fanciful or deceptive. The imagery conveys the idea of being faced with numerous options, leading to feelings of confusion, indecision, or being overwhelmed by possibilities.

Psychologically, The Seven of Cups represents the challenge of discernment and the allure of illusions. It signifies the mind's capacity to envision possibilities but also its vulnerability to deception and wishful thinking. In readings, The Seven of Cups suggests a period of introspection to differentiate between viable options and deceptive fantasies. It encourages the querent to clarify their goals and make choices grounded in reality. This card resonates with the Jungian concept of confronting the myriad aspects of the subconscious and the need to sift through them to find true direction and purpose.

The presence of The Seven of Cups in a spread signals a time to carefully evaluate one's choices. It encourages the querent to distinguish between realistic goals and illusory desires, to avoid getting lost in fantasies, and to focus on practical decision-making.

When reversed, The Seven of Cups may suggest emerging from a state of confusion, gaining clarity, or the realization that some dreams are unattainable. It might indicate the need to ground oneself in reality and make more informed and realistic decisions.

Through Carl Jung's theories, The Seven of Cups represents the exploration of the unconscious and its many facets. It embodies the psychological journey of sifting through inner desires, fears, and dreams to uncover one's true motivations and goals.

"The Seven of Cups" symbolizes the complexities of choice and the seductive power of illusion. It personifies the process of navigating through a maze of options, emphasizing the need for discernment and the careful evaluation of one's desires and aspirations. The card suggests that understanding the difference between fantasy and reality is crucial for making wise choices and achieving genuine fulfillment.

Multiplicity of Choices: The Seven of Cups highlights the abundance of choices and opportunities available. It suggests the importance of careful consideration and the avoidance of hasty decisions.

Illusions and Wishful Thinking: The card emphasizes the allure of illusions and the temptation of wishful thinking. It encourages a realistic assessment of options to avoid being misled by fantasies.

Discernment and Decision-Making: The Seven of Cups is often associated with the challenge of discernment in decision-making. It invites evaluating each option's viability and aligning choices with one's true goals.

Overwhelm and Confusion: The card suggests that an excess of options can lead to confusion and indecisiveness. It encourages simplifying one's choices to focus on what truly matters.

The Seven of Cups as a Symbol of Imagination: In readings, The Seven of Cups often represents the power of imagination and the creative exploration of possibilities.

Clarity and Realization: When reversed, The Seven of Cups can indicate gaining clarity from confusion or realizing the impracticality of certain dreams, prompting a more grounded approach.

The Seven of Cups in Personal Growth: In the context of personal growth, The Seven of Cups symbolizes the journey of exploring one's inner world of desires and fears to understand better what drives one's choices and actions.

"The Seven of Cups" serves as a profound reminder of the need for discernment amidst life's abundant choices. It encourages navigating the realm of possibilities with wisdom and clarity, distinguishing between what is genuinely fulfilling and what is mere illusion, thereby guiding one towards making decisions that lead to authentic happiness and achievement.

Eight of Cups

"The Eight of Cups," a card in the Minor Arcana of tarot decks, symbolizes abandonment, withdrawal, and the search for deeper meaning. This card typically depicts a figure walking away from eight cups stacked unevenly, signifying leaving behind something that no longer serves a purpose or fulfills emotionally. The solitary journey into a barren landscape or towards a mountain under a moonlit sky represents a quest for something more meaningful, suggesting a journey of self-discovery or spiritual seeking.

Psychologically, The Eight of Cups represents the difficult decision to move on from familiar circumstances or relationships that have become unfulfilling. It signifies the emotional courage required to seek greater fulfillment, even in the face of uncertainty. In readings, The Eight of Cups suggests a period of introspection and decision-making, urging the querent to follow their inner call towards a more authentic path, even if it means leaving comfort behind. This card resonates with the Jungian concept of individuation, where one embarks on a journey of self-realization, often leading to the abandonment of previous identities or situations.

The presence of The Eight of Cups in a spread signals a time of emotional transition and the need for change. It encourages the querent to let go of outdated attachments and to pursue a path that aligns more closely with their deeper needs and aspirations.

When reversed, The Eight of Cups may suggest reluctance to move on, fear of the unknown, or an incomplete emotional journey. It might indicate the need to reevaluate one's reasons for staying and to consider if the fear of change is preventing personal growth.

Through Carl Jung's theories, The Eight of Cups represents the journey of delving into the unconscious to discover one's true desires and motivations. It embodies the psychological process of leaving behind what is known in pursuit of a more authentic and fulfilling life.

"The Eight of Cups" symbolizes the bravery involved in abandoning the known for the unknown. It personifies the quest for deeper meaning and fulfillment, emphasizing the importance of heeding one's inner call and embracing the journey towards self-discovery. The card suggests that true emotional and spiritual growth often requires stepping out of one's comfort zone and exploring new horizons.

Emotional Transition and Letting Go: The Eight of Cups highlights the importance of emotional transition and the process of letting go. It suggests that moving on from unfulfilling situations is necessary for growth.

Search for Deeper Meaning: The card emphasizes the search for deeper meaning and fulfillment. It encourages exploring one's inner world and seeking a path that aligns with true personal values.

Courage to Embrace Change: The Eight of Cups is often associated with the courage required to embrace change. It invites stepping into the unknown in pursuit of a more authentic life.

Inner Call and Self-Realization: The card suggests following one's inner call towards self-realization. It advocates listening to one's inner voice and making decisions that reflect one's true self.

The Eight of Cups as a Symbol of Personal Journey: In readings, The Eight of Cups often represents a personal journey of discovery, where the querent is prompted to leave behind the old to seek new experiences.

Fear of the Unknown: When reversed, The Eight of Cups can indicate a fear of stepping into the unknown or reluctance to leave behind the familiar, suggesting a need to address these fears for personal growth.

The Eight of Cups in Personal Development: In the context of personal development, The Eight of Cups symbolizes the journey of introspection and the pursuit of a more meaningful and fulfilling path.

"The Eight of Cups" serves as a powerful reminder of the significance of pursuing one's true path. It encourages embracing the emotional journey of letting go and moving forward, recognizing that the pursuit of deeper understanding and fulfillment often requires leaving behind what is known and comfortable.

Nine of Cups

"The Nine of Cups," a card in the Minor Arcana of tarot decks, symbolizes contentment, satisfaction, and emotional fulfillment. This card is often depicted with a figure seated comfortably before a table on which nine cups are arranged. The figure's demeanor suggests a sense of pride and fulfillment, representing the achievement of emotional or personal desires. The cups, often seen as symbols of emotional experiences, are upright and full, indicating that the querent's wishes or aspirations have been realized.

Psychologically, The Nine of Cups represents a state of emotional well-being, where one feels content and satisfied with their achievements. It signifies the fulfillment of desires, emotional stability, and the enjoyment of life's pleasures. In readings, The Nine of Cups suggests a period of happiness and contentment, where the querent's wishes are coming to fruition. This card resonates with the Jungian concept of achieving a sense of completeness and satisfaction in one's emotional life.

The presence of The Nine of Cups in a spread signals a time of joy and fulfillment. It encourages the querent to savor their achievements, to feel proud of their emotional journey, and to enjoy the sense of well-being that comes from contentment and satisfaction.

When reversed, The Nine of Cups may suggest unfulfilled wishes, dissatisfaction, or taking one's blessings for granted. It might indicate the need to reassess what truly brings happiness or to consider whether the pursuit of personal desires has neglected other important aspects of life.

Through Carl Jung's theories, The Nine of Cups represents the harmonization of the emotional self, achieving a state of inner contentment and satisfaction. It embodies the psychological journey of recognizing and appreciating one's emotional accomplishments and the fulfillment of personal desires.

"The Nine of Cups" symbolizes the realization of emotional wishes and the joy of contentment. It personifies the achievement of a stable and satisfying emotional state, emphasizing the importance of recognizing and valuing one's emotional journey. The card suggests that acknowledging and celebrating one's emotional successes is key to a sense of fulfillment and happiness.

Emotional Satisfaction and Well-being: The Nine of Cups highlights the importance of emotional satisfaction and well-being. It suggests a time of enjoying the fruits of one's emotional labor and feeling content with life's accomplishments.

Fulfillment of Desires: The card emphasizes the fulfillment of personal desires and aspirations. It encourages appreciating the achievements and the journey that led to them.

Enjoyment and Pleasure: The Nine of Cups is often associated with enjoyment and pleasure. It invites indulging in life's joys and celebrating the happiness that comes from emotional stability.

Gratitude and Appreciation: The card suggests a focus on gratitude and appreciation for what one has achieved. It encourages recognizing and being thankful for life's blessings.

The Nine of Cups as a Symbol of Achievement: In readings, The Nine of Cups often represents the achievement of goals and the satisfaction that comes from realizing personal dreams and wishes.

Balancing Desires and Responsibilities: When reversed, The Nine of Cups can indicate the need to balance personal desires with other responsibilities or to reassess what truly brings happiness.

The Nine of Cups in Personal Development: In the context of personal development, The Nine of Cups symbolizes the journey towards achieving emotional goals and the satisfaction that comes from personal growth and emotional maturity.

"The Nine of Cups" serves as a powerful reminder of the joy that comes from emotional fulfillment and the realization of personal desires. It encourages embracing contentment, celebrating achievements, and appreciating the journey towards emotional satisfaction and well-being.

Ten of Cups

"The Ten of Cups," a card in the Minor Arcana of tarot decks, symbolizes emotional abundance, familial harmony, and the realization of lasting happiness. This card typically depicts a joyful family scene, with figures looking at a rainbow adorned with ten cups. The imagery of the rainbow and the contented family unit conveys a sense of fulfillment, unity, and emotional prosperity. The cups in the sky represent the culmination of emotional goals and the attainment of a harmonious and joyful domestic life.

Psychologically, The Ten of Cups represents the achievement of emotional stability and satisfaction within one's personal relationships, particularly within the family or close community. It signifies a state of enduring happiness and contentment, where emotional needs are met, and relationships are harmonious and nurturing. In readings, The Ten of Cups suggests a period of joyous family life, emotional fulfillment, and the realization of personal dreams within the context of supportive relationships. This card resonates with the Jungian concept of individuation achieved not in isolation but within the fabric of meaningful relationships, contributing to a sense of wholeness and belonging.

The presence of The Ten of Cups in a spread signals a time of relational harmony and emotional fulfillment. It encourages the querent to cherish and nurture their family and community relationships, recognizing the deep satisfaction and joy these connections bring.

When reversed, The Ten of Cups may suggest disharmony, disconnection, or unfulfilled emotional aspirations within one's relationships. It might indicate the need to address issues within the family or community to restore harmony and emotional well-being.

Through Carl Jung's theories, The Ten of Cups represents the collective aspect of emotional fulfillment, highlighting the importance of relationships and community in achieving a sense of completeness and happiness. It embodies the psychological journey of building and maintaining fulfilling relationships that contribute to one's overall sense of well-being and emotional health.

"The Ten of Cups" symbolizes the ultimate achievement in emotional contentment and relational harmony. It personifies the joy of family and community bonds, emphasizing the importance of nurturing and cherishing these connections. The card suggests that true emotional fulfillment often lies in the quality and depth of one's relationships and the shared happiness within a supportive and loving community.

Emotional Fulfillment and Joy: The Ten of Cups highlights the importance of emotional fulfillment and joy, especially within the context of family and close relationships. It suggests a time of happiness and contentment derived from loving connections.

Harmony in Relationships: The card emphasizes harmony and unity in personal relationships. It encourages fostering a loving and supportive environment within the family and community.

Celebration of Family Life: The Ten of Cups is often associated with a celebration of family life and domestic bliss. It invites cherishing and appreciating the joy and stability that come from close familial bonds.

Realization of Emotional Goals: The card suggests the realization of emotional goals and aspirations, particularly in the realm of personal relationships and home life.

The Ten of Cups as a Symbol of Wholeness: In readings, The Ten of Cups often represents a state of wholeness and completeness achieved through harmonious relationships and emotional satisfaction.

Addressing Relationship Issues: When reversed, The Ten of Cups can indicate the need to address and resolve issues within family or community relationships to achieve emotional harmony.

The Ten of Cups in Personal Growth: In the context of personal growth, The Ten of Cups symbolizes the journey towards creating and maintaining fulfilling relationships that contribute significantly to one's sense of emotional well-being and happiness.

"The Ten of Cups" serves as a powerful reminder of the joy and fulfillment found in loving relationships and a harmonious home life. It encourages building and nurturing strong family and community bonds, recognizing that these connections are integral to one's emotional health and overall happiness.

Page of Cups

"The Page of Cups," a card in the Minor Arcana of tarot decks, symbolizes curiosity, emotional openness, and the beginnings of creative or emotional journeys. This card often depicts a young figure, the Page, holding a cup from which a fish is seen emerging. This imagery represents the unexpected and imaginative aspects of emotions, symbolizing a youthful and open attitude towards emotional and creative experiences. The fish leaping from the cup signifies intuitive insights and the birth of creative ideas or feelings.

Psychologically, The Page of Cups represents the exploration of emotions and the willingness to embrace new feelings or creative inspirations. It signifies a period of emotional growth, where one is open to experiencing and expressing emotions in a fresh and unencumbered way. In readings, The Page of Cups suggests a time of emotional curiosity and exploration, encouraging the querent to trust their feelings and to be receptive to the emotional and creative messages emerging from within. This card resonates with the Jungian concept of the 'puer aeternus' or eternal youth, embodying the spirit of openness, wonder, and exploration that is often associated with youth.

The presence of The Page of Cups in a spread signals a time to embrace emotional and creative beginnings. It encourages the querent to remain open to new emotional experiences, to explore their intuition, and to express their feelings with the innocence and purity often found in youth.

When reversed, The Page of Cups may suggest emotional immaturity, daydreaming, or being overly fanciful. It might indicate the need to ground one's emotional and creative impulses in reality and to approach feelings and inspirations with a balance of openness and practicality.

Through Carl Jung's theories, The Page of Cups represents the initial stages of emotional development and the exploration of the unconscious mind. It embodies the psychological process of discovering and integrating emerging feelings and creative impulses, forming a more nuanced and complete emotional self.

"The Page of Cups" symbolizes the freshness of emotional and creative beginnings. It personifies the exploratory nature of the human psyche in the realm of emotions and creativity, emphasizing the importance of approaching life with curiosity, openness, and a willingness to experience and express feelings in their purest form. The card suggests that embracing one's emotional and creative intuition is key to personal growth and emotional development.

Emotional Exploration and Openness: The Page of Cups highlights the significance of emotional exploration and maintaining an open heart. It suggests a time of discovering new emotional landscapes and expressing feelings authentically.

Creative Beginnings and Intuition: The card emphasizes the importance of creative beginnings and following one's intuition. It encourages trusting in spontaneous ideas and inspirations as sources of creative expression.

Innocence and Purity in Expression: The Page of Cups is often associated with the innocence and purity found in youth. It invites expressing emotions and creativity with honesty and without preconceived judgments.

Receptivity to Emotional Messages: The card suggests being receptive to emotional messages and insights. It encourages paying attention to the subconscious mind and the messages it conveys through feelings and dreams.

The Page of Cups as a Symbol of Potential: In readings, The Page of Cups often represents the potential for emotional and creative growth. It signifies the early stages of emotional development and the joy of discovering one's emotional depth.

Balancing Imagination and Reality: When reversed, The Page of Cups can indicate the need to balance imagination with practicality, ensuring that dreams and emotions are grounded in reality.

The Page of Cups in Personal Growth: In the context of personal growth, The Page of Cups symbolizes the journey of exploring and integrating new emotional aspects, contributing to a richer and more diverse emotional self.

"The Page of Cups" serves as a powerful reminder of the value of approaching emotions and creativity with a sense of wonder and openness. It encourages exploring the depths of one's feelings and creative impulses, embracing the journey of emotional discovery, and expressing oneself with the freshness and honesty characteristic of youth.

Knight of Cups

"The Knight of Cups," a card in the Minor Arcana of tarot decks, epitomizes the archetype of the romantic, artistic seeker. This card often portrays a knight gracefully riding a horse, holding a cup as a symbol of his quest for emotional and artistic fulfillment. The calm horse represents controlled emotions, while the knight's focused gaze suggests a deep commitment to his emotional or creative pursuits.

Psychologically, The Knight of Cups represents the exploration of emotional depths and the pursuit of ideals. This knight embodies the enthusiasm for new emotional experiences and the journey to understand and express deep feelings. In readings, The Knight of Cups suggests a time to embrace romantic or creative aspirations, to be open to love, and to pursue emotional goals with sincerity and dedication. The card resonates with the Jungian concept of integrating the anima or animus, reflecting a harmonious balance of masculine and feminine energies in the pursuit of emotional and artistic expression.

The presence of The Knight of Cups in a spread signals an invitation to follow one's heart with idealism and passion. It encourages the querent to approach emotional experiences with authenticity and to express their feelings artistically and gracefully.

When reversed, The Knight of Cups may indicate emotional naivety, unrealistic romantic expectations, or being swayed excessively by feelings. It suggests a need for grounding idealistic pursuits in reality and approaching emotions with maturity and discernment.

Through Carl Jung's theories, The Knight of Cups represents the journey towards emotional and artistic actualization. Unlike the Page who embarks on initial exploration, the Knight symbolizes a deeper, more mature engagement with the emotional and creative realms. It embodies the psychological process of reconciling idealistic dreams with the complexities of real emotional experiences, navigating the journey with a blend of imagination and emotional intelligence.

"The Knight of Cups" symbolizes the quest for emotional and artistic truth. It personifies the pursuit of ideals in love and art, emphasizing the value of following one's heart with both passion and thoughtfulness. The card suggests that a mature, emotionally balanced approach to life's romantic and creative aspects is key to personal fulfillment and meaningful expression.

Embracing Emotional and Artistic Pursuits: The Knight of Cups highlights the importance of embracing emotional depth and artistic expression, encouraging a pursuit driven by heartfelt passion and creativity.

Idealism in Love and Creativity: The card emphasizes idealism in love and creative endeavors. It invites experiencing and expressing emotions with depth, sincerity, and an artistic flair.

Emotional Maturity and Intelligence: Unlike the youthful impulsiveness of the Page, The Knight of Cups suggests a more mature and emotionally intelligent approach to pursuits of the heart and creativity.

Navigating Emotional Landscapes: The Knight of Cups is often associated with navigating complex emotional landscapes, balancing idealism with the realities of emotional experiences.

The Knight of Cups as a Symbol of Emotional Depth: In readings, The Knight of Cups often represents a journey into the depths of emotion and creativity, exploring these realms with a balanced and thoughtful approach.

Balancing Dreams with Reality: When reversed, The Knight of Cups can highlight the need to balance dreams and idealism with practicality and emotional maturity, ensuring that pursuits are realistic and grounded.

The Knight of Cups in Personal Growth: In the context of personal development, The Knight of Cups symbolizes the evolution from initial emotional exploration to a deeper, more nuanced engagement with one's feelings and creative impulses.

"The Knight of Cups" serves as a reminder of the richness of pursuing one's emotional and artistic aspirations with depth and maturity. It encourages a harmonious blend of imagination and emotional intelligence in the quest for love, artistic expression, and emotional fulfillment.

Queen of Cups

"The Queen of Cups," a card in the Minor Arcana of tarot decks, symbolizes emotional depth, intuition, and compassionate understanding. This card is often depicted with a queen sitting by the water, holding a decorative cup that is sometimes closed, symbolizing her deep connection with her own emotions and the subconscious. The water around her represents the realm of emotions, and her calm demeanor reflects a mastery over feelings, suggesting a person who is empathetic and nurturing.

Psychologically, The Queen of Cups represents the nurturing aspect of the emotional self. She signifies emotional intelligence, empathy, and the ability to connect deeply with others. In readings, The Queen of Cups suggests a time to trust your intuition, to be compassionate with yourself and others, and to embrace the depth of your emotional experiences. This card resonates with the Jungian archetype of the 'Great Mother,' embodying qualities of care, understanding, and emotional stability.

The presence of The Queen of Cups in a spread signals a period where emotional insight and compassionate understanding are needed. It encourages the querent to embrace empathy, to trust their intuitive feelings, and to offer emotional support to themselves and others.

When reversed, The Queen of Cups may suggest being overly emotional, moody, or out of touch with one's intuition. It might indicate the need to balance emotional involvement with practicality and to ensure that empathy does not turn into over-sensitivity or co-dependency.

Through Carl Jung's theories, The Queen of Cups represents the integration of the emotional and nurturing aspects of the psyche. She embodies the psychological process of understanding and harmonizing the emotional self, achieving a balance between deep emotional understanding and practical, everyday life.

"The Queen of Cups" symbolizes the embodiment of emotional wisdom and nurturing. She personifies the qualities of emotional depth, intuition, and empathy, emphasizing the importance of understanding and expressing feelings with maturity and compassion. The card suggests that developing emotional insight and a caring approach to oneself and others is integral to personal growth and well-being.

Emotional Depth and Understanding: The Queen of Cups highlights the importance of emotional depth and understanding. She encourages exploring the depths of your feelings and being open to the emotional experiences of others.

Intuitive Insight: The card emphasizes the value of intuition and inner wisdom. It suggests trusting your instincts and using your emotional intelligence to navigate life's challenges.

Nurturing and Empathy: The Queen of Cups is often associated with nurturing and empathetic qualities. She invites offering care and understanding to those in need, as well as practicing self-compassion.

Balance in Emotional Expressions: The Queen of Cups suggests finding a balance in expressing emotions. She advocates for handling feelings with grace and maturity, without repressing or being overwhelmed by them.

The Queen of Cups as a Symbol of Emotional Stability: In readings, The Queen of Cups often represents emotional stability and the ability to offer wise counsel and support based on deep emotional understanding.

Maintaining Emotional Boundaries: When reversed, The Queen of Cups can indicate the need to maintain emotional boundaries, ensuring that empathy and care do not lead to emotional drain or loss of self-identity.

The Queen of Cups in Personal Growth: In the context of personal development, The Queen of Cups symbolizes the journey towards becoming emotionally wise and nurturing, integrating one's emotional depth with the ability to care for and understand others effectively.

"The Queen of Cups" serves as a powerful reminder of the strength found in emotional wisdom and nurturing. She encourages embracing the depth of one's emotions, offering empathy and understanding, and using intuitive insight to enrich both personal growth and the well-being of others.

King of Cups

"The King of Cups," a card in the Minor Arcana of tarot decks, embodies emotional maturity, wisdom, and a deep understanding of the human psyche. This card typically portrays a regal figure seated on a throne amidst turbulent waters, holding a cup and a scepter, signifying a command over emotions and the ability to navigate through complex emotional landscapes with calm and stability. The sea represents the vastness of the emotional realm, while the king's composed demeanor reflects his mastery in managing feelings and relationships with equanimity.

Psychologically, The King of Cups represents the integration of emotional intelligence with leadership and authority. He signifies the capacity to remain emotionally balanced and compassionate, even in challenging situations. In readings, The King of Cups suggests a time to lead with empathy, to offer guidance from a place of understanding, and to manage one's emotions with wisdom and maturity. This card resonates with the Jungian archetype of the wise ruler or healer, embodying qualities of emotional depth, understanding, and the responsible use of power in guiding others.

The presence of The King of Cups in a spread signals a period where emotional leadership and wisdom are called for. It encourages the querent to approach situations with empathy, to maintain emotional stability, and to use their emotional insight to lead and support others effectively.

When reversed, The King of Cups may suggest emotional manipulation, moodiness, or being out of touch with one's emotional self. It might indicate the need to reassess one's approach to emotional management and to ensure that emotional wisdom is used for constructive and benevolent purposes.

Through Carl Jung's theories, The King of Cups represents the mature development of the emotional self. He embodies the psychological journey of achieving emotional equilibrium and using this balance to guide and heal, reflecting a deep understanding of the human condition and the complexities of emotions.

"The King of Cups" symbolizes the pinnacle of emotional intelligence and control. He personifies the ideal of emotional leadership, emphasizing the importance of navigating life's challenges with empathy, understanding, and psychological insight. The card suggests that true leadership and wisdom come from a deep understanding of emotions, both one's own and those of others, and the responsible application of this knowledge.

Emotional Wisdom and Balance: The King of Cups highlights the importance of emotional wisdom and balance. He encourages cultivating an understanding of emotions and using this knowledge to maintain stability in various life aspects.

Empathetic Leadership: The card emphasizes the value of leading with empathy and understanding. It suggests using emotional intelligence to guide, support, and influence others positively.

Navigating Complex Emotions: The King of Cups is often associated with the skill of navigating complex emotional situations. He invites maintaining composure and a balanced perspective, even in turbulent emotional waters.

Mastery over Emotional Realm: The King of Cups suggests a mastery over the emotional realm. He advocates for using emotional depth and stability to create harmony and understanding in relationships and situations.

The King of Cups as a Symbol of Emotional Authority: In readings, The King of Cups often represents a figure of emotional authority and wisdom, offering guidance and support based on a deep understanding of the human psyche.

Responsible Use of Emotional Insight: When reversed, The King of Cups can indicate the need to review the use of emotional power and insight, ensuring that it is applied responsibly and ethically.

The King of Cups in Personal Development: In the context of personal development, The King of Cups symbolizes the journey towards achieving emotional maturity and using one's emotional capabilities to positively impact others and oneself.

"The King of Cups" serves as a powerful reminder of the strength found in emotional intelligence and empathy. He encourages leading with compassion, understanding the complexities of the emotional world, and using emotional wisdom to guide oneself and others toward stability, harmony, and understanding.

The Pentacles Series
Ace of Pentacles

"The Ace of Pentacles," a card in the Minor Arcana of tarot decks, symbolizes opportunity, prosperity, and new financial or material beginnings. This card typically depicts a hand emerging from a cloud, holding a large, shining pentacle or coin, signifying the manifestation of material opportunities and the potential for tangible success. The landscape below often includes a lush garden or pathway leading through an archway, representing the journey towards material and physical security.

Psychologically, The Ace of Pentacles represents the realization of practical goals and the potential for building a stable and secure foundation. It signifies the initial stages of material or financial ventures, where the groundwork for future success is laid. In readings, The Ace of Pentacles suggests a time to seize material opportunities, to invest in practical endeavors, and to focus on building a solid foundation for future growth. This card resonates with the Jungian concept of individuation, as it reflects the process of manifesting one's potential in the physical world and achieving a sense of security and groundedness.

The presence of The Ace of Pentacles in a spread signals a period ripe for material growth and the initiation of successful ventures. It encourages the querent to pursue tangible goals, to take advantage of opportunities for financial or physical advancement, and to lay the groundwork for lasting stability and prosperity.

When reversed, The Ace of Pentacles may suggest missed opportunities, financial delays, or challenges in manifesting material goals. It might indicate the need to reassess one's approach to financial or physical matters and to ensure that the foundation of one's ventures is strong and practical.

Through Carl Jung's theories, The Ace of Pentacles represents the integration of the physical and material aspects of life with one's personal growth. It embodies the psychological journey of grounding one's aspirations in reality and creating tangible results from one's efforts and potential.

"The Ace of Pentacles" symbolizes the promise of material success and the opportunity to build a stable and prosperous future. It personifies the beginning of fruitful endeavors in the material realm, emphasizing the importance of practicality, planning, and seizing opportunities for physical and financial growth. The card suggests that embracing practical opportunities and focusing on material stability are key steps in achieving overall personal fulfillment and security.

Manifestation of Material Goals: The Ace of Pentacles highlights the importance of manifesting material goals. It suggests seizing opportunities to build a secure and stable foundation for future growth.

Opportunity for Prosperity: The card emphasizes the potential for prosperity and success in financial or physical endeavors. It encourages taking practical steps towards achieving material objectives.

Groundwork for Future Success: The Ace of Pentacles is often associated with laying the groundwork for future success. It invites careful planning and investment in solid ventures.

Realization of Potential: The card suggests realizing one's potential in the material world. It encourages turning aspirations and abilities into tangible achievements.

The Ace of Pentacles as a Symbol of New Beginnings: In readings, The Ace of Pentacles often represents new beginnings in financial, physical, or material aspects, indicating a fresh start with promising prospects.

Practicality and Material Focus: When reversed, The Ace of Pentacles can indicate the need to reassess material goals and approaches, focusing on practicality and realistic planning.

The Ace of Pentacles in Personal Development: In the context of personal development, The Ace of Pentacles symbolizes the journey towards achieving material stability and success, integrating practical goals with personal growth and stability.

"The Ace of Pentacles" serves as a powerful reminder of the opportunities and potential in the material world. It encourages embracing practical endeavors, focusing on material and financial stability, and laying a strong foundation for future success and prosperity.

Two of Pentacles

"The Two of Pentacles," a card in the Minor Arcana of tarot decks, embodies the concept of balance, adaptability, and the juggling of life's demands. It typically depicts a figure skillfully balancing two pentacles within an infinity symbol, illustrating the continuous effort required to manage multiple responsibilities. The turbulent sea in the background further underscores the need for flexibility in the face of changing circumstances.

Psychologically, this card reflects the human capacity to handle fluctuating situations and the balancing act between various aspects of life, such as work, finances, and personal affairs. It signifies the art of multitasking and maintaining equilibrium amidst life's ups and downs. In readings, The Two of Pentacles suggests a phase where balance and adept handling of responsibilities are essential. It encourages the querent to remain flexible, to adapt to changing situations, and to manage resources and energy efficiently. This card resonates with Jung's concept of the balance between the conscious and unconscious mind, navigating life's complexities with agility and awareness.

The appearance of The Two of Pentacles in a spread signals a time of fluctuation and the need for skillful balance. It urges the querent to stay adaptable, maintain a sense of humor, and manage their time and resources adeptly.

When reversed, The Two of Pentacles may suggest a significant imbalance, feeling overwhelmed by life's demands, or a struggle to maintain flexibility. It might indicate a period where the querent is overextended, trying to juggle too much, which leads to stress or burnout. This reversal calls for a reassessment of priorities, potentially simplifying commitments, or seeking more efficient ways to handle tasks. It also suggests that the querent might be resisting change, clinging to outdated routines, or failing to acknowledge the need for a new approach to balance their responsibilities. The reversed Two of Pentacles asks for a thorough evaluation of how tasks and challenges are being managed. It may be a time to delegate, to say no to additional responsibilities, and to understand the limits of one's capacity to avoid adverse consequences on physical and emotional well-being.

Through Carl Jung's theories, The Two of Pentacles represents the psychological agility required to maintain balance amidst opposing forces and demands. It embodies adapting to life's changing dynamics while preserving inner stability and external poise.

"The Two of Pentacles" symbolizes life's balancing act. It personifies managing various tasks and responsibilities, emphasizing the importance of adaptability, resourcefulness, and maintaining equilibrium. The card suggests that navigating life's fluctuations requires a blend of flexibility, practicality, and a light-hearted approach.

Three of Pentacles

"The Three of Pentacles" symbolizes the power of collaboration and the pursuit of excellence. It personifies the commitment to craftsmanship and the value of bringing together diverse talents and viewpoints. The card suggests that cooperation, shared goals, and dedication to quality are key to achieving success and realizing one's potential.

Collaborative Efforts and Teamwork: The Three of Pentacles highlights the significance of collaborative efforts and teamwork. It suggests that bringing together diverse skills and perspectives enhances the quality of work.

Commitment to Quality: The card emphasizes the importance of a commitment to quality and excellence. It encourages refining skills and paying attention to detail in all endeavors.

Learning and Skill Development: The Three of Pentacles is often associated with learning and applying skills in a practical context. It invites continuous improvement and the application of one's abilities to achieve high standards.

Mutual Respect in Teamwork: The card suggests the importance of mutual respect and effective communication in collaborative efforts. It advocates for valuing each person's contribution and working cohesively towards a common goal.

The Three of Pentacles as a Symbol of Mastery: In readings, The Three of Pentacles often represents the process of working towards mastery and excellence, both individually and as part of a team.

Addressing Collaboration Challenges: When reversed, The Three of Pentacles can highlight challenges in teamwork, suggesting a need to reassess collaboration strategies, improve communication, and focus on collective goals.

The Three of Pentacles in Personal Growth: In the context of personal development, The Three of Pentacles symbolizes the journey of mastering one's craft and the importance of integrating individual talents with those of others to create something meaningful and exceptional.

"The Three of Pentacles" serves as a powerful reminder of the value of collaboration, skill, and dedication to quality. It encourages engaging in teamwork with a spirit of learning, sharing expertise, and striving for the highest standards in all endeavors.

Four of Pentacles

"The Four of Pentacles," a card in the Minor Arcana of tarot decks, symbolizes security, control, and possession, often with an emphasis on the material aspect. This card typically depicts a figure tightly holding onto four pentacles, representing a desire for financial stability and fear of loss. The figure's posture, clutching one pentacle closely to the chest and balancing others with feet and head, illustrates a protective stance over resources and achievements.

Psychologically, The Four of Pentacles reflects a mindset focused on safeguarding assets and maintaining control over one's environment. It signifies a preoccupation with material security and can suggest resistance to change due to fear of financial instability or loss. In readings, The Four of Pentacles suggests a period where the querent may be overly concerned with material possessions or financial security, potentially leading to rigidity or a reluctance to share and open up. This card resonates with the Jungian concept of the shadow self, where the fear of instability can lead to behaviors driven by insecurity and the need for control.

The presence of The Four of Pentacles in a spread signals a time to evaluate one's relationship with material possessions and financial control. It urges the querent to consider the balance between security and openness, and to beware of becoming too guarded or miserly.

When reversed, The Four of Pentacles may suggest a loosening of one's grip on material possessions, an opening to sharing and generosity, or the potential consequences of being overly fixated on material security. It might indicate the need to release excessive control, to trust more in the flow of life, and to cultivate a more open and generous attitude towards resources.

Through Carl Jung's theories, The Four of Pentacles represents the challenge of confronting and integrating aspects of the psyche that are overly attached to security and control. It embodies the psychological journey of balancing material concerns with emotional and spiritual well-being.

"The Four of Pentacles" symbolizes the dual nature of material security. It personifies the human desire for stability and the potential pitfalls of attachment and control. The card suggests that while it is important to value and manage one's resources effectively, an excessive focus on material security can lead to emotional and spiritual constriction.

Focus on Material Security: The Four of Pentacles highlights the importance of material security and the management of resources. It suggests carefully considering financial decisions and the need for stability.

Guarding Against Loss: The card emphasizes a protective stance towards assets and achievements. It invites considering the balance between safeguarding resources and being open to change and growth.

Risk of Rigidity and Miserliness: The Four of Pentacles is often associated with rigidity and a reluctance to share or let go. It warns against the potential downsides of being overly fixated on material control.

Evaluating Financial Attitudes: The card suggests evaluating one's attitudes towards wealth and possessions. It encourages reflection on the impact of these attitudes on overall well-being.

The Four of Pentacles as a Symbol of Stability: In readings, The Four of Pentacles often represents a desire for financial stability and control, but also cautions against the limitations of being too possessive or resistant to change.

Opening to Generosity: When reversed, The Four of Pentacles can indicate a shift towards more generosity and openness, or the need to let go of excessive control over material matters.

The Four of Pentacles in Personal Development: In the context of personal development, The Four of Pentacles symbolizes the journey of understanding and balancing one's material needs with emotional and spiritual aspects, recognizing that true security encompasses more than just financial or physical assets.

"The Four of Pentacles" serves as a reminder of the need for balance in our approach to material possessions and financial stability. It encourages a mindful and balanced perspective on wealth and resources, promoting a healthy integration of material concerns with broader life values and goals.

Five of Pentacles

"The Five of Pentacles," a card in the Minor Arcana of tarot decks, evokes themes of hardship, scarcity, and the feeling of being left out in the cold. This card typically features two figures, often depicted as destitute or in despair, walking through snow outside a stained-glass window, symbolizing isolation and unmet needs. The window suggests the presence of warmth and comfort nearby, yet out of reach, underscoring a sense of exclusion and unfulfilled desires.

Psychologically, The Five of Pentacles represents experiences of lack, whether material, emotional, or spiritual. It signifies periods of struggle, where individuals may feel unsupported, neglected, or facing financial hardships. In readings, The Five of Pentacles suggests a time to acknowledge feelings of loss or deprivation and to seek support or new solutions. This card resonates with the Jungian concept of the 'shadow,' reflecting aspects of life that are often ignored or suppressed, such as poverty, rejection, and the need for community support.

The presence of The Five of Pentacles in a spread calls attention to the need for compassion and support during challenging times. It encourages the querent to seek help, to recognize the value of community resources, and to be mindful of the needs of others who might be facing similar struggles.

When reversed, The Five of Pentacles may suggest emerging from a period of hardship, finding new resources, or a change in perspective about one's circumstances. It might indicate the need to break free from a mindset of scarcity, to foster a sense of abundance, and to be open to new opportunities for support and improvement.

Through Carl Jung's theories, The Five of Pentacles represents the confrontation with societal and personal shadows, such as poverty and exclusion. It embodies the psychological journey of facing difficult circumstances, the feeling of being an outsider, and the search for healing and integration in both personal and community contexts.

"The Five of Pentacles" symbolizes the challenges of scarcity and the feeling of being marginalized. It personifies the human experience of facing adversity, emphasizing the importance of seeking support, community, and new perspectives. The card suggests that navigating through times of hardship requires resilience, the willingness to ask for help, and the recognition of shared human experiences.

Experiences of Lack and Hardship: The Five of Pentacles underscores the reality of experiencing lack, whether it's financial hardship, emotional deprivation, or spiritual emptiness.

Seeking Support and Resources: The card highlights the importance of seeking support and utilizing available resources during times of need. It encourages reaching out for help and finding strength in community connections.

Feeling of Exclusion and Neglect: The Five of Pentacles is often associated with feelings of exclusion, neglect, and being overlooked by society. It invites awareness and compassion for those who are marginalized.

Recognition of Shared Struggles: The card suggests recognizing shared human struggles and the value of empathy and support in overcoming adversities.

The Five of Pentacles as a Symbol of Resilience: In readings, The Five of Pentacles often represents resilience in the face of adversity, encouraging the querent to find inner strength and seek supportive communities.

Changing Perspectives on Scarcity: When reversed, The Five of Pentacles can indicate a shift in perspective from scarcity to potential abundance. It suggests a reevaluation of one's situation and the discovery of new paths to improvement.

The Five of Pentacles in Personal Growth: In the context of personal development, The Five of Pentacles symbolizes the journey of overcoming hardship and developing a deeper understanding of one's needs and the needs of others in the community.

"The Five of Pentacles" serves as a reminder of the challenges that come with scarcity and the feeling of exclusion. It encourages seeking support, fostering resilience, and cultivating a compassionate perspective towards oneself and others facing adversity.

Six of Pentacles

"The Six of Pentacles," a card in the Minor Arcana of tarot decks, represents generosity, fairness, and the balance of resources. This card is typically depicted with a figure, often seen as wealthy or in a position of power, distributing coins to the needy, while holding a balanced scale. The imagery signifies the act of giving and receiving, highlighting the importance of charity, financial balance, and the equitable distribution of wealth.

Psychologically, The Six of Pentacles explores the dynamics of power and dependency in relationships, particularly regarding financial or material assistance. It signifies the need for kindness and generosity, as well as the responsibility that comes with possessing resources or power. In readings, The Six of Pentacles suggests a period where the querent may be in a position to offer help or might be in need of assistance. It encourages the practice of generosity, with mindfulness towards fairness and the dignity of all involved. This card resonates with the Jungian idea of the balance between the ego and the shadow, in the context of material wealth and the ethical implications of its use and distribution.

The presence of The Six of Pentacles in a spread calls for an assessment of one's financial situation, encouraging the sharing of resources if one is able, or the seeking of help if in need. It urges the querent to consider the flow of give-and-take in their life and to approach financial transactions with fairness and empathy.

When reversed, The Six of Pentacles may suggest issues of unfairness, one-sided generosity, or dependency in financial matters. It might highlight the need to reassess the balance of giving and receiving, to address inequalities, or to avoid using financial aid as a means of control.

Through Carl Jung's theories, The Six of Pentacles represents the integration of one's attitudes towards wealth and generosity, balancing personal needs with those of the community. It embodies the psychological journey of understanding the impact of one's financial decisions on both the self and the broader society.

"The Six of Pentacles" symbolizes the delicate balance of generosity and fairness. It personifies the act of giving with compassion and receiving with gratitude, emphasizing the ethical implications of wealth and resource distribution. The card suggests that true balance in life involves not only managing one's finances wisely but also understanding the importance of generosity and the responsibility that comes with wealth.

Generosity and Fairness: The Six of Pentacles highlights the importance of generosity and fairness in financial dealings. It encourages sharing resources with those in need while maintaining a sense of equity.

Dynamics of Giving and Receiving: The card emphasizes the balance between giving and receiving. It invites an exploration of how one manages their resources and the impact of their financial decisions on others.

Ethical Use of Wealth: The Six of Pentacles is often associated with the ethical use of wealth and power. It suggests using financial resources responsibly and with consideration for the broader community.

Balance of Power in Financial Relationships: The card underscores the need to maintain a balance of power in financial relationships, ensuring that generosity does not turn into dependency or control.

The Six of Pentacles as a Symbol of Material Responsibility: In readings, The Six of Pentacles often represents the responsibility that comes with material wealth, emphasizing the need for thoughtful and fair distribution of resources.

Reassessing Financial Ethics: When reversed, The Six of Pentacles can indicate a need to reassess one's approach to financial aid, addressing issues of dependency, fairness, or the misuse of financial power.

The Six of Pentacles in Personal Development: In the context of personal development, The Six of Pentacles symbolizes the journey of understanding and integrating one's relationship with money, considering both personal needs and the impact of financial decisions on others.

"The Six of Pentacles" serves as a reminder of the importance of kindness and equitable distribution in financial matters. It encourages a thoughtful and compassionate approach to wealth, emphasizing the value of fairness and generosity in achieving a balanced and ethical life.

Seven of Pentacles

"The Seven of Pentacles," a card in the Minor Arcana of tarot decks, symbolizes patience, long-term planning, and the assessment of progress. This card typically depicts a figure taking a rest from tending a garden, gazing contemplatively at the growing pentacles on the plants, representing investments or efforts that are yet to fully mature. The imagery conveys the importance of hard work, the need for patience during growth periods, and the value of pausing to evaluate one's progress and strategy.

Psychologically, The Seven of Pentacles explores the themes of perseverance and the anticipation of rewards from one's endeavors. It signifies the reflective phase in any venture where one assesses the fruits of their labor and considers the next steps. In readings, The Seven of Pentacles suggests a period of waiting and evaluating before the next phase of action, encouraging the querent to be patient and to analyze their efforts and strategies. This card resonates with the Jungian concept of individuation, reflecting the process of growth and development, where periodic reflection and assessment are crucial for personal and professional success.

The presence of The Seven of Pentacles in a spread signals a time of evaluation and anticipation. It urges the querent to practice patience, to reflect on their progress, and to plan their next moves wisely, considering the long-term implications of their actions.

When reversed, The Seven of Pentacles may suggest impatience, dissatisfaction with progress, or a need to reassess one's approach. It might indicate frustration with the pace of development or a warning against short-sighted or hasty decisions. This reversal calls for a reassessment of goals and methods, encouraging the querent to find more effective ways to achieve their objectives.

Through Carl Jung's theories, The Seven of Pentacles represents the psychological journey of growth, patience, and introspection. It embodies the process of assessing one's development, reevaluating goals, and cultivating the patience required for meaningful and lasting achievements.

"The Seven of Pentacles" symbolizes the thoughtful pause in the journey of effort and achievement. It personifies the need for patience and strategic planning, emphasizing the value of taking stock of one's progress and preparing for future steps. The card suggests that growth often requires time and reflection, and that careful consideration and patience are key to realizing one's aspirations.

Patience and Long-Term Planning: The Seven of Pentacles underscores the importance of patience and strategic planning for long-term success. It encourages an understanding that meaningful achievements often take time to develop.

Assessment of Progress: The card highlights the value of periodically assessing one's progress and efforts. It invites taking a step back to evaluate achievements and to recalibrate goals and strategies.

Reflection During Growth Phases: The Seven of Pentacles is often associated with reflective pauses during periods of growth. It suggests recognizing and appreciating the incremental progress made in any venture.

Anticipation of Future Rewards: The card suggests a period of anticipation and expectation of future rewards from current efforts.

It encourages maintaining focus and dedication during the growth process.

The Seven of Pentacles as a Symbol of Development: In readings, The Seven of Pentacles often represents a phase of development where patience and careful planning are essential for the fruition of one's efforts.

Reevaluation and Adaptation: When reversed, The Seven of Pentacles can indicate a need to reevaluate current approaches or to adapt strategies to better align with one's goals, especially when faced with delays or obstacles.

The Seven of Pentacles in Personal Development: In the context of personal development, The Seven of Pentacles symbolizes the journey of cultivating patience, introspection, and strategic thinking in the pursuit of one's objectives.

"The Seven of Pentacles" serves as a reminder of the benefits of patience, reflection, and careful planning in achieving one's goals. It encourages a thoughtful and measured approach to endeavors, highlighting the importance of persistence and strategic foresight in personal and professional growth.

Eight of Pentacles

"The Eight of Pentacles," a card in the Minor Arcana of tarot decks, exemplifies dedication, mastery, and attention to detail in one's work or craft. This card often portrays an artisan intently focused on crafting pentacles, each one a testament to skill, persistence, and the pursuit of excellence. The repetitive nature of the task highlights the importance of practice and perseverance in achieving high standards and expertise.

Psychologically, The Eight of Pentacles represents the value of hard work, the dedication to honing one's skills, and the satisfaction derived from diligent effort and improvement. It signifies a period of intense focus and commitment to one's craft or career, underscoring the importance of a strong work ethic and continuous learning. In readings, The Eight of Pentacles suggests a time for putting in the effort to refine one's abilities, to focus on the task at hand, and to take pride in the meticulous execution of work. This card resonates with the Jungian concept of individuation through the mastery of one's skills, reflecting the process of personal development and self-realization through dedicated work and craftsmanship.

The presence of The Eight of Pentacles in a spread signals a phase of skill development and diligent work. It encourages the querent to embrace the process of learning, to concentrate on their work, and to appreciate the value of persistence and meticulous effort.

When reversed, The Eight of Pentacles may suggest a lack of focus, a waning in dedication, or dissatisfaction with one's work or progress. It might indicate the need to rediscover passion for one's work, to reassess work-life balance, or to address issues of perfectionism or overworking.

Through Carl Jung's theories, The Eight of Pentacles represents the integration of skills and hard work with one's personal journey. It embodies the psychological process of developing competence and the deepening of one's understanding of their craft or profession.

"The Eight of Pentacles" symbolizes the virtues of diligence, commitment, and skillful execution. It personifies the process of becoming proficient in one's work, emphasizing the importance of dedication, attention to detail, and continuous improvement. The card suggests that true fulfillment and success in any field are achieved through sustained effort, dedication to craftsmanship, and a continuous pursuit of excellence.

Dedication to Craftsmanship: The Eight of Pentacles highlights the importance of dedication to one's craft or profession. It encourages a commitment to continuous improvement and skill development.

Value of Hard Work: The card emphasizes the value of hard work and meticulous effort. It suggests taking pride in one's work and the process of achieving excellence through persistence.

Focus and Concentration: The Eight of Pentacles is often associated with intense focus and concentration on the task at hand. It invites immersing oneself in their work and paying attention to every detail.

Pursuit of Mastery: The card suggests the pursuit of mastery and expertise in one's field. It encourages refining skills and striving for the highest standards in one's work.

The Eight of Pentacles as a Symbol of Improvement: In readings, The Eight of Pentacles often represents a phase of skill enhancement and work ethic. It signifies a commitment to becoming the best in one's chosen field.

Addressing Work-Life Balance: When reversed, The Eight of Pentacles can indicate a need to reassess one's approach to work, addressing issues such as overworking, perfectionism, or lack of fulfillment.

The Eight of Pentacles in Personal Development: In the context of personal development, The Eight of Pentacles symbolizes the journey of honing one's abilities and the satisfaction that comes from skillful and purposeful work.

"The Eight of Pentacles" serves as a reminder of the rewards of dedication and hard work. It encourages embracing the journey of skill development, focusing on quality and craftsmanship, and finding fulfillment in the process of continuous learning and improvement in one's work.

Nine of Pentacles

"The Nine of Pentacles," a card in the Minor Arcana of tarot decks, epitomizes self-reliance, abundance, and the enjoyment of success. This card often features an elegant figure, surrounded by a lush garden, with a bird of prey perched on their hand. The imagery conveys a sense of luxury, comfort, and the fruits of one's labor. The garden symbolizes the cultivation of personal goals, and the bird represents freedom and intelligence, suggesting mastery over one's life.

Psychologically, The Nine of Pentacles reflects the achievement of independence and the enjoyment of the benefits of one's hard work. It signifies self-sufficiency, financial stability, and the ability to enjoy the finer things in life, achieved through personal effort and discipline. In readings, The Nine of Pentacles suggests a period of enjoying the rewards of hard work, encouraging the querent to appreciate their achievements and to savor the comfort and security they have earned. This card resonates with the Jungian concept of individuation, where an individual achieves a sense of fulfillment and self-actualization, having successfully integrated various aspects of their personality.

The presence of The Nine of Pentacles in a spread signals a time of personal fulfillment and financial stability. It encourages the querent to relish their achievements, to enjoy the comfort they have created for themselves, and to value their independence and self-reliance.

When reversed, The Nine of Pentacles may suggest over-dependence on material comforts, isolation, or a lack of fulfillment despite material wealth. It might indicate the need to reconnect with others, to find joy beyond material possessions, or to address feelings of complacency.

Through Carl Jung's theories, The Nine of Pentacles represents the culmination of a journey towards self-reliance and personal success. It embodies the psychological process of realizing one's potential and achieving a harmonious balance between material success and personal well-being.

"The Nine of Pentacles" symbolizes the gratification of achieving self-sufficiency and enjoying one's own successes. It personifies the attainment of a comfortable and independent life, emphasizing the importance of enjoying the results of one's hard work and discipline. The card suggests that true satisfaction comes from achieving stability through one's efforts and enjoying the personal freedom and security that comes with it.

Personal Fulfillment and Independence: The Nine of Pentacles underscores the achievement of personal fulfillment and independence. It encourages enjoying the results of one's hard work and valuing self-sufficiency.

Enjoyment of Comforts and Success: The card emphasizes the enjoyment of comforts and successes earned through personal effort. It invites savoring the pleasures and stability that one has created.

Self-Reliance and Financial Stability: The Nine of Pentacles is often associated with self-reliance and financial stability. It suggests the importance of managing one's resources wisely to maintain independence.

Appreciation of Luxuries and Achievements: The card suggests appreciating the luxuries and achievements in life. It encourages gratitude for the material and personal accomplishments.

The Nine of Pentacles as a Symbol of Achievement: In readings, The Nine of Pentacles often represents the culmination of efforts and the attainment of a stable, comfortable lifestyle.

Reevaluating Material Fulfillment: When reversed, The Nine of Pentacles can indicate a need to reevaluate one's relationship with material comforts, addressing issues of isolation or a lack of fulfillment.

The Nine of Pentacles in Personal Development: In the context of personal development, The Nine of Pentacles symbolizes the journey towards achieving independence and enjoying the fruits of one's labor, finding a balance between material success and personal contentment.

"The Nine of Pentacles" serves as a reminder of the rewards of diligence and self-reliance. It encourages appreciating and enjoying the success and comfort one has achieved, while also remaining mindful of the value of personal connections and inner fulfillment beyond material wealth.

Ten of Pentacles

"The Ten of Pentacles," a card in the Minor Arcana of tarot decks, symbolizes wealth, legacy, and long-term success. It often depicts a multi-generational family, with elderly figures, children, and sometimes pets, amidst a luxurious estate adorned with pentacles. This imagery represents the culmination of wealth and stability achieved over a lifetime, encompassing family, financial security, and the legacy passed down through generations.

Psychologically, The Ten of Pentacles reflects the fulfillment of material goals and the establishment of a lasting legacy. It signifies stability, not just in financial terms but also in creating a foundation for future generations. In readings, The Ten of Pentacles suggests a time of enjoying the rewards of long-term efforts, encouraging the querent to think about their legacy and the long-term impact of their actions. This card resonates with the Jungian concept of completeness, where an individual achieves not only material success but also a sense of fulfillment through contributing to the well-being of their family and community.

The presence of The Ten of Pentacles in a spread signals a phase of stability and the fruition of long-term plans. It urges the querent to appreciate the security they have built and to consider the legacy they are creating, both materially and in the values they impart.

When reversed, The Ten of Pentacles may suggest issues with family inheritance, instability in long-term plans, or a lack of satisfaction despite material wealth. It might indicate the need to address family dynamics, to reassess one's long-term goals, or to find fulfillment beyond material success.

Through Carl Jung's theories, The Ten of Pentacles represents the integration of material success with personal and familial well-being. It embodies the psychological journey of building a legacy that transcends mere financial wealth, encompassing family values, traditions, and long-term stability.

"The Ten of Pentacles" symbolizes the achievement of holistic success. It personifies the realization of long-term stability and prosperity, emphasizing the importance of building a lasting legacy and contributing to the welfare of future generations. The card suggests that true wealth is measured not only in financial terms but also in the lasting impact one has on their family and community.

Long-Term Stability and Success: The Ten of Pentacles underscores the importance of long-term stability and success. It encourages planning and working towards a secure future for oneself and one's family.

Family Legacy and Wealth: The card emphasizes the concept of family legacy and the transfer of wealth, knowledge, and values across generations. It invites consideration of the impact and legacy one wishes to leave behind.

Holistic Approach to Wealth: The Ten of Pentacles is often associated with a holistic approach to wealth, incorporating financial security and the richness of family and tradition.

Appreciation of Fulfilled Goals: The card suggests appreciating the fulfillment of long-term goals and the comfort of stability. It encourages gratitude for the security and prosperity achieved.

The Ten of Pentacles as a Symbol of Completion: In readings, The Ten of Pentacles often represents the culmination of efforts in building a lasting legacy and achieving comprehensive success in life's various aspects.

Challenges in Wealth and Legacy: When reversed, The Ten of Pentacles can indicate challenges related to wealth, family inheritance, or dissatisfaction with the established order. It suggests addressing these issues to ensure a stable and harmonious legacy.

The Ten of Pentacles in Personal Development: In the context of personal development, The Ten of Pentacles symbolizes the journey towards creating and enjoying a life of wealth, stability, and familial harmony, balancing material success with personal values and family relationships.

"The Ten of Pentacles" serves as a reminder of the value of long-term planning, family bonds, and the creation of a legacy that extends beyond material wealth. It encourages a comprehensive approach to success, valuing stability, family, and tradition as integral components of a fulfilling life.

Page of Pentacles

The Page of Pentacles typically depicts a young figure, standing in a field with a singular pentacle in their hands. They gaze at it with fascination and curiosity, embodying a sense of wonder and the eagerness to learn. The landscape around them is usually lush and fertile, indicating that the seeds of their ambitions are ready to be planted and nurtured.

The Page of Pentacles represents the initial stages of engagement with the material world. This card signifies an eagerness to learn about tangible realities, be it in the realm of finance, education, or practical skills. The Page stands for youthfulness not just in age but in attitude – a mindset open to learning, exploration, and laying the foundations for future success. In readings, this card suggests a period of study, apprenticeship, or the beginning of a new business venture or financial plan. It resonates with the Jungian archetype of the 'eternal student' – always curious, seeking knowledge, and open to growth.

When the Page of Pentacles appears in a spread, it's a call to embrace new learning opportunities and to approach your financial and practical goals with curiosity and dedication. This card encourages grounding your dreams in reality and taking tangible steps towards achieving them. It signifies a time to be diligent, focused, and to invest in yourself through education, skill-building, or careful financial planning.

When reversed, the Page of Pentacles might suggest a lack of focus, procrastination, or ungrounded ambitions. It could indicate that you are either too focused on the minutiae, leading to inaction, or you are daydreaming without implementing practical steps. It's a nudge to reevaluate your approach, encouraging a more structured or realistic path to achieving your goals.

In the context of personal development, the Page of Pentacles symbolizes the journey of learning and growth. It's about understanding the value of patience, persistence, and practicality. The card represents the building blocks of character and competence, emphasizing the importance of a solid foundation in any endeavor.

The Page of Pentacles thus serves as a potent symbol of potential and possibility. It represents the beginning of a journey towards material and intellectual fulfillment, reminding us that every expert was once a beginner, and every grand ambition starts with a simple, well-planned step.

Knight of Pentacles

"The Knight of Pentacles," a card in the Minor Arcana of tarot decks, symbolizes diligence, reliability, and a methodical approach to life's tasks. This card is often depicted as a knight, clad in armor, seated upon a sturdy horse and holding a single pentacle. Unlike the knights of other suits, this knight appears stationary, suggesting a character of steadfastness, careful planning, and unwavering focus.

Psychologically, The Knight of Pentacles represents the attributes of persistence, responsibility, and thoroughness. It signifies a person who approaches tasks with seriousness and a strong work ethic, preferring a steady and measured approach to quick or impulsive actions. In readings, this card suggests a time for being dependable and meticulous in your endeavors, encouraging the querent to pursue their goals with endurance and attention to detail. The Knight of Pentacles resonates with the Jungian concept of the 'earthly warrior', embodying the virtues of steadfastness, reliability, and a deep connection to the physical world.

The presence of The Knight of Pentacles in a spread indicates a period where thoroughness and methodical approaches are favored. It encourages the querent to remain grounded, to plan carefully, and to commit to their tasks with a dedication to quality and completion.

When reversed, The Knight of Pentacles may suggest stagnation, a lack of progress, or an overly cautious approach. It might indicate the need to infuse some dynamism into your efforts, to balance careful planning with action, or to overcome a tendency towards procrastination or inflexibility.

Through Carl Jung's theories, The Knight of Pentacles represents the integration of steadfastness and practicality in one's personality. It embodies the psychological journey of pursuing goals with dedication and a realistic approach, emphasizing the importance of staying connected to practical realities.

"The Knight of Pentacles" symbolizes the virtues of reliability, thoroughness, and persistence. It personifies the commitment to a methodical and steady approach in life's endeavors, emphasizing the importance of patience, planning, and practicality in achieving success. The card suggests that the most reliable path to success is often through persistent effort, careful planning, and a steadfast commitment to one's goals.

Reliability and Thoroughness: The Knight of Pentacles highlights the importance of reliability and thoroughness in pursuits. It encourages a consistent and dependable approach to tasks and responsibilities.

Persistence and Methodical Approach: The card emphasizes the value of persistence and a methodical approach in achieving goals. It suggests that steady progress often leads to lasting success.

Commitment to Quality: The Knight of Pentacles is often associated with a commitment to quality and attention to detail. It invites maintaining high standards and a dedication to excellence in your work.

Grounded and Practical Actions: The card suggests adopting grounded and practical actions in pursuit of goals. It encourages a realistic and well-planned approach to tasks.

The Knight of Pentacles as a Symbol of Steadfastness: In readings, The Knight of Pentacles often represents a phase of steady progress and reliability, emphasizing the benefits of a diligent and methodical approach.

Balancing Caution with Action: When reversed, The Knight of Pentacles can indicate a need to balance caution with proactive steps, addressing issues of stagnation or inflexibility.

The Knight of Pentacles in Personal Development: In the context of personal development, The Knight of Pentacles symbolizes the journey of developing and integrating qualities of reliability, thoroughness, and practicality, fostering a dependable and grounded approach to life's challenges.

"The Knight of Pentacles" serves as a reminder of the power of steadfastness and diligence in life's journey. It encourages adopting a reliable, thorough, and methodical approach to tasks, highlighting the value of persistence and practicality in achieving long-term success and fulfillment.

Queen of Pentacles

"The Queen of Pentacles," a card in the Minor Arcana of tarot decks, epitomizes nurturing abundance, resourcefulness, and a grounded approach to life's material aspects. This card typically depicts a queen seated in a lush, verdant landscape, holding a pentacle, symbolizing her connection with the earth and her ability to manifest material security and comfort.

Psychologically, The Queen of Pentacles represents the embodiment of practical wisdom, stability, and a nurturing presence. She signifies a person who is not only successful in managing material resources but also provides support and care in a down-to-earth manner. In readings, this card suggests a period where you may be called upon to use your practical skills to nurture yourself and others, encouraging the querent to balance material pursuits with a warm and caring approach. The Queen of Pentacles resonates with the Jungian archetype of the 'earth mother', representing fertility, abundance, and the grounding of one's energy in practical endeavors.

The presence of The Queen of Pentacles in a spread signals a time of stability and comfort. It urges the querent to embrace their nurturing side, to tend to the physical needs of themselves and others, and to utilize their practical skills for the betterment of all.

When reversed, The Queen of Pentacles may suggest a neglect of the physical aspects of life, overindulgence, or a disconnection from one's nurturing nature. It might indicate the need to refocus on creating balance between material wealth and the well-being of oneself and others.

Through Carl Jung's theories, The Queen of Pentacles represents the integration of material success with emotional and physical well-being. It embodies the psychological process of nurturing not just financial growth but also the growth and care of oneself and those around.

"The Queen of Pentacles" symbolizes the strength found in nurturing, stability, and practicality. It personifies the harmonious management of material wealth and resources, emphasizing the importance of a caring and grounded approach in all material matters. The card suggests that true wealth includes not only financial success but also the creation of a stable, nurturing environment for oneself and others.

Nurturing Abundance and Practical Wisdom: The Queen of Pentacles underscores the importance of nurturing abundance and applying practical wisdom in everyday life. It encourages caring for physical needs with a sensible, grounded approach.

Balancing Material and Emotional Needs: The card emphasizes the balance between material success and emotional well-being. It invites creating a harmonious environment that supports both financial stability and personal care.

Resourcefulness and Stability: The Queen of Pentacles is often associated with resourcefulness and the ability to create stability and comfort. It suggests using one's practical abilities to enhance life's material aspects.

Caring and Grounded Presence: The card suggests embodying a caring and grounded presence, offering support and stability to those around you.

The Queen of Pentacles as a Symbol of Comfort: In readings, The Queen of Pentacles often represents a period of comfort and stability, emphasizing the nurturing of oneself and others.

Reassessing Material Focus: When reversed, The Queen of Pentacles can indicate a need to reassess one's approach to material wealth, ensuring that it doesn't overshadow the importance of emotional and physical care.

The Queen of Pentacles in Personal Development: In the context of personal development, The Queen of Pentacles symbolizes the journey towards achieving material stability while maintaining a nurturing and practical approach to life's challenges.

"The Queen of Pentacles" serves as a reminder of the power of practical wisdom and nurturing in creating a life of abundance. It encourages a balanced and caring approach to material wealth, highlighting the importance of stability, resourcefulness, and a nurturing presence in achieving overall well-being.

King of Pentacles

"The King of Pentacles," a card in the Minor Arcana of tarot decks, represents the epitome of success, stability, and mastery over the material and business realms. This card typically portrays a regal figure seated amidst a scene of abundant prosperity, holding the symbol of a pentacle, signifying wealth, success, and material accomplishment.

Psychologically, The King of Pentacles symbolizes a person who has achieved a high level of success in the material world and is adept at managing financial and business affairs. This character is not only wealthy but also wise in the ways of sustaining and growing wealth. The King embodies reliability, efficiency, and a practical approach to life's material aspects. In readings, this card suggests a period of financial stability and the wise management of resources, encouraging the querent to make practical decisions and to use their skills and experience to build and maintain stability. The King of Pentacles resonates with the Jungian archetype of the wise ruler, someone who is responsible, dependable, and grounded in reality.

The presence of The King of Pentacles in a spread signals a time of material success and the effective management of practical affairs. It urges the querent to embrace a pragmatic approach to their financial and material goals, often indicating the ability to achieve prosperity through hard work and wise investments.

When reversed, The King of Pentacles may suggest a misuse of wealth or skills, materialistic attitudes, or a lack of connection to the more emotional or spiritual aspects of life. It might indicate the need to reassess one's approach to wealth and material possessions, to find a balance between the material and other life aspects.

Through Carl Jung's theories, The King of Pentacles represents the successful integration of material wisdom and practical skills. It embodies the psychological journey of achieving and maintaining material stability, symbolizing the maturity and responsibility required to handle wealth and resources effectively.

"The King of Pentacles" symbolizes the zenith of material achievement and stability. It personifies the mastery over financial and business matters, emphasizing the importance of a grounded, practical approach to achieving and sustaining success. The card suggests that true mastery in the material world comes not just from the accumulation of wealth, but also from the wise and ethical management of resources, and the ability to use one's success for the benefit of others.

Mastery of Material Success: The King of Pentacles underscores the mastery of financial and material success, encouraging the effective management of resources and wealth.

Practical and Grounded Leadership: The card emphasizes practical and grounded leadership in business and financial matters. It invites making wise decisions based on experience and practical knowledge.

Wealth and Responsibility: The King of Pentacles is often associated with wealth and the responsibility that comes with managing it. It suggests using one's resources wisely and ethically.

Material Wisdom: The card suggests embodying material wisdom, achieving success through hard work, and practical strategies.

Balanced Approach to Wealth: When reversed, The King of Pentacles can indicate the need for a more balanced approach to wealth, avoiding materialistic attitudes and ensuring a holistic view of success.

The King of Pentacles in Personal Development: In the context of personal development, The King of Pentacles symbolizes the journey towards achieving material stability and using one's skills and knowledge for responsible and ethical wealth management.

"The King of Pentacles" serves as a reminder of the virtues of practical wisdom, responsible leadership, and ethical management in the realm of material success. It encourages embracing a balanced and grounded approach to financial and business affairs, ensuring that material success is achieved and sustained through wise, responsible, and ethical means.

The Sword Series

Ace of swords

"The Ace of Swords," a card in the Minor Arcana of tarot decks, embodies the emergence of intellect, clarity, and breakthroughs. This card often depicts a hand emerging from a cloud, firmly grasping a double-edged sword that points skyward. The sword's crown at the tip symbolizes victory and mental clarity, while surrounding yods represent divine inspiration or enlightenment.

Psychologically, The Ace of Swords signifies the power of a clear, sharp mind and the breakthroughs that come from intellectual revelations. It represents a moment of clarity or an epiphany, where truth cuts through confusion and ambiguity. In readings, this card suggests a time for clear thinking, decisive action, and speaking one's truth. It encourages the querent to use their intellect and reason to navigate through challenges, symbolizing a breakthrough or a new understanding. The Ace of Swords resonates with the Jungian archetype of the 'sword of truth', cutting through deceit and illusion to reveal the heart of the matter.

The presence of The Ace of Swords in a spread indicates a period of mental clarity and the beginning of new intellectual endeavors. It suggests the importance of honest communication, clear thinking, and the power of truth and justice.

When reversed, The Ace of Swords may suggest confusion, miscommunication, or the misuse of intellectual power. It might indicate clouded judgment, a lack of clarity, or the need to cut through deception to find the truth.

Through Carl Jung's theories, The Ace of Swords represents the integration of intellect and truth. It embodies the psychological journey of achieving clarity, discernment, and the realization of one's intellectual potential.

"The Ace of Swords" symbolizes the triumph of clarity and intellect. It personifies the onset of mental sharpness and the power of clear communication, emphasizing the importance of using one's intellect to achieve understanding and justice. The card suggests that clarity, truth, and intellectual breakthroughs are crucial for overcoming obstacles and achieving one's goals.

Clarity of Thought and Communication: The Ace of Swords underscores the importance of clarity of thought and communication. It encourages using one's intellect and reason to navigate life's challenges.

Breakthroughs and New Understandings: The card emphasizes the potential for breakthroughs and new understandings. It suggests being open to moments of clarity and epiphanies that can change one's perspective.

Intellectual Power and Justice: The Ace of Swords is often associated with intellectual power and the pursuit of justice. It invites the use of mental acuity to discern truth and uphold fairness.

Honesty and Truth: The card suggests the importance of honesty and speaking one's truth. It encourages clear, direct communication and standing up for one's beliefs.

The Ace of Swords as a Symbol of New Beginnings: In readings, The Ace of Swords often represents new intellectual endeavors, the beginning of a journey of clarity and understanding.

Addressing Miscommunication and Confusion: When reversed, The Ace of Swords can indicate a need to address miscommunication or confusion, urging a reevaluation of one's thought processes and communication methods.

The Ace of Swords in Personal Development: In the context of personal development, The Ace of Swords symbolizes the journey of developing intellectual clarity and using one's mind to cut through illusion and achieve greater understanding.

"The Ace of Swords" serves as a reminder of the power of the mind and the value of intellectual clarity. It encourages embracing truth, clarity, and justice, and using intellectual strength to overcome obstacles and achieve a deeper understanding of oneself and the world around.

Two of Swords

"The Two of Swords," a card in the Minor Arcana of tarot decks, epitomizes the complexities of decision-making, inner conflict, and the delicate balance of opposing forces. Often depicted is a blindfolded figure seated with crossed swords, symbolizing a stalemate or equilibrium that must be addressed. The blindfold implies a need for inner reflection to make a choice, suggesting that the answer lies within rather than in external cues.

Psychologically, The Two of Swords represents a moment of indecision and the tension of opposing thoughts or feelings. It signifies the challenge of making a balanced decision when clear direction is obscured, and emotions and intellect are at odds. In readings, this card often indicates a need for calm and detachment to gain clarity, suggesting a temporary withdrawal from the situation to better understand the underlying issues. The Two of Swords resonates with the Jungian concept of the reconciliation of opposites, highlighting the necessity of inner balance and harmony in resolving external conflicts.

The presence of The Two of Swords in a spread signals a critical junction, where contemplation and impartial judgment are key. It encourages the querent to seek serenity and neutrality in their thought process, emphasizing the importance of not rushing into a decision without a clear understanding.

When reversed, The Two of Swords might suggest that a decision has been made hastily, without proper consideration, or that there is an avoidance of facing the reality of a situation. It can highlight the need to confront one's indecision or ambivalence, urging a more engaged and decisive approach to resolve the impasse.

"The Two of Swords" thus stands as a symbol of the intellectual and emotional equilibrium required in decision-making. It personifies the challenge of navigating through uncertainty with a balanced and reflective approach, underscoring the importance of inner peace and objectivity in resolving dilemmas. The card encourages a thoughtful, introspective approach to decision-making, advocating for a balance between intuition and rational thought in navigating life's complex choices.

Decisive Balance and Inner Conflict: The Two of Swords highlights the importance of balancing opposing forces within oneself, finding equilibrium in decision-making amidst internal conflict.

Objective Reflection and Detachment: The card emphasizes the need for objective reflection and detachment. It invites pausing and considering all aspects before making a decision.

Reconciliation of Opposites: The Two of Swords is often associated with the reconciliation of opposing thoughts or emotions, suggesting the necessity of inner harmony for external resolution.

Contemplation in Decision-Making: The card suggests the importance of contemplation and neutrality in decision-making, urging the querent to seek clarity through introspection.

The Two of Swords as a Symbol of Indecision: In readings, The Two of Swords often represents a stalemate or impasse, highlighting the challenges and complexities in making a pivotal decision.

Addressing Avoidance and Hasty Decisions: When reversed, The Two of Swords can indicate the consequences of avoidance or hasty decisions, emphasizing the need for a more thorough and engaged approach to decision-making.

The Two of Swords in Personal Development: In the context of personal development, The Two of Swords symbolizes the journey of achieving mental clarity and emotional balance, fostering a more holistic and thoughtful approach to resolving life's dilemmas.

"The Two of Swords" serves as a reminder of the intricacies and nuances in decision-making processes. It encourages embracing a balanced and introspective approach to resolving dilemmas, highlighting the importance of inner peace, objectivity, and thoughtful consideration in navigating life's challenging decisions.

Three of Swords

"The Three of Swords," a striking card in the Minor Arcana of tarot decks, conveys themes of heartache, sorrow, and emotional pain. This card is typically depicted with three swords piercing a heart, symbolizing the deep impact of loss, betrayal, or a painful realization. The often-stormy background in the imagery emphasizes the turbulent emotional landscape that accompanies such experiences.

Psychologically, The Three of Swords embodies the process of confronting and working through emotional pain. It signifies moments of grief, sadness, or disappointment, where the heart experiences the sharp sting of life's harsher realities. In readings, this card suggests a time of emotional difficulty, encouraging the querent to face and process their feelings honestly. It is a reminder that while pain is an inevitable part of life, it also offers opportunities for growth and deeper understanding. The Three of Swords resonates with the Jungian concept of confronting the shadow self, acknowledging the parts of our experience that we may find difficult to accept but are essential for personal growth and healing.

The presence of The Three of Swords in a spread is an indication to address emotional wounds head-on. It urges the querent to acknowledge the pain they are experiencing, to understand its source, and to begin the healing process.

When reversed, The Three of Swords may suggest the beginning of healing from past hurts, or it may warn of lingering emotional wounds that have not been fully addressed. It can indicate the need for further emotional work to move past grief and find closure.

"The Three of Swords" thus symbolizes the challenging yet necessary journey through emotional pain and heartbreak. It personifies the experience of dealing with difficult emotions, emphasizing the importance of confronting and processing feelings to pave the way for healing and personal growth. The card encourages a courageous and honest exploration of emotional pain, understanding that such experiences, while difficult, are crucial for emotional depth and resilience.

Emotional Pain and Heartbreak: The Three of Swords underscores the reality of emotional pain and heartbreak, highlighting the importance of facing and processing these feelings.

Confrontation with Difficult Emotions: The card emphasizes the necessity of confronting difficult emotions, suggesting that acknowledging and understanding these feelings is crucial for healing.

Journey Through Grief: The Three of Swords is often associated with the journey through grief and disappointment, representing the emotional challenges that accompany loss and betrayal.

Opportunities for Growth: Despite its somber tone, the card suggests that pain and sorrow can be transformative, offering opportunities for deeper self-understanding and emotional growth.

Healing and Recovery: When reversed, The Three of Swords can signify the beginning of healing, indicating that the querent is starting to move past emotional pain and finding ways to recover.

The Three of Swords in Personal Development: In the context of personal development, The Three of Swords symbolizes the process of working through emotional pain, learning valuable lessons about resilience, and gaining emotional depth through difficult experiences.

"The Three of Swords" serves as a poignant reminder of the complexities of the human heart. It encourages embracing the full spectrum of emotional experiences, recognizing that while heartache is challenging, it is an integral part of the journey towards emotional maturity and depth.

Four of Swords

"The Four of Swords," a card in the Minor Arcana of tarot decks, signifies a period of rest, contemplation, and recuperation. This card is often illustrated with a figure lying in repose, as if in a state of retreat or meditation, with three swords hanging above and one beneath them. This imagery represents a time of stillness and mental recovery, suggesting a break from conflict or stress.

Psychologically, The Four of Swords symbolizes the need for mental and emotional respite. It acknowledges the importance of taking a step back from life's battles to rejuvenate and gain perspective. In readings, this card often indicates a period of recovery after a time of challenge, urging the querent to take time for self-care and mental rest. It encourages finding peace and clarity through solitude and reflection. The Four of Swords resonates with the Jungian concept of withdrawal from the external world to attend to the inner self, highlighting the necessity of periods of rest for psychological balance and renewal.

The presence of The Four of Swords in a spread is a call to embrace a period of healing and quietude. It suggests the importance of allowing oneself time to recharge, both mentally and emotionally, especially after periods of stress or conflict.

When reversed, The Four of Swords may suggest a prolonged period of inactivity or a resistance to returning to action. It might indicate restlessness or an urge to re-engage with the world, signaling that the period of rest has served its purpose, and it is time to wake from repose.

"The Four of Swords" thus symbolizes the crucial role of rest and contemplation in maintaining mental and emotional health. It personifies the need for a retreat from life's demands, emphasizing the importance of finding a sanctuary of peace to recharge and gain clarity. The card encourages a mindful approach to rest, understanding that such periods are not merely passive but are active phases of healing, reflection, and psychological rejuvenation.

Rest and Recuperation: The Four of Swords underscores the importance of rest and recuperation for mental and emotional well-being. It encourages taking a break from life's demands to recharge.

Contemplation and Reflection: The card emphasizes the value of contemplation and reflection. It suggests using this time of rest to gain perspective and clarity on past events and future direction.

Period of Healing: The Four of Swords is often associated with a period of healing, particularly after a time of stress or conflict. It invites embracing stillness and quietude for recovery.

Mental and Emotional Renewal: The card suggests a phase of mental and emotional renewal, advocating for a temporary withdrawal from external activities to focus on inner peace and balance.

Transition Back to Activity: When reversed, The Four of Swords can indicate readiness to transition back to activity, suggesting that the querent has rested enough and is now prepared to re-engage with their daily life.

The Four of Swords in Personal Development: In the context of personal development, The Four of Swords symbolizes the journey of understanding the need for mental breaks and the value of solitude in fostering personal growth and clarity.

"The Four of Swords" serves as a reminder of the power of restorative stillness. It encourages honoring the need for mental and emotional breaks as essential parts of the journey towards self-awareness, balance, and renewed strength.

Five of Swords

"The Five of Swords," a card in the Minor Arcana of tarot decks, represents conflict, defeat, and the hollow victory. This card typically features a solitary figure holding swords, with other figures retreating in the background, symbolizing a scenario where one wins at the expense of others, or a situation where no true victory is possible.

Psychologically, The Five of Swords speaks to the mindset of winning at all costs, often leading to pyrrhic victories where the win is not worth the price paid. It signifies moments of conflict, aggression, and unethical behavior, highlighting the consequences of such actions. In readings, this card often suggests a period of strife or tension, encouraging the querent to consider the implications of their actions and the potential for unnecessary conflict. It urges reflection on whether the pursuit of victory is causing more harm than good. The Five of Swords resonates with the Jungian shadow aspect, where the darker elements of competition and aggression come to the forefront.

The presence of The Five of Swords in a spread is an indication to reassess one's approach to conflict and competition. It suggests the importance of considering the broader impact of one's actions and whether the pursuit of individual goals is damaging relationships or personal integrity.

When reversed, The Five of Swords may suggest a release from conflict or a realization that continuing a battle is futile. It might indicate a desire to seek resolution or to move past a period of hostility, suggesting a shift towards reconciliation or a more cooperative approach.

"The Five of Swords" thus symbolizes the complex nature of conflict and competition. It personifies the challenges of navigating situations where ethical boundaries may be tested, emphasizing the importance of considering the consequences of one's actions. The card encourages a thoughtful approach to conflict, advocating for strategies that foster harmony and understanding, rather than aggression and division.

Conflict and Aggression: The Five of Swords underscores the themes of conflict and aggression, highlighting the potential for ethical dilemmas and the consequences of hostile actions.

Reflection on Victory and Defeat: The card emphasizes the need to reflect on what constitutes a true victory, questioning the value of winning at the expense of others.

Consideration of Consequences: The Five of Swords is often associated with the broader impact of one's actions, inviting a consideration of how pursuit of personal goals may affect others.

Shift Toward Resolution: When reversed, The Five of Swords can indicate a move away from conflict and towards resolution, suggesting a reevaluation of the need for aggression or competition.

The Five of Swords in Personal Development: In the context of personal development, The Five of Swords symbolizes the journey of understanding the complexities of conflict and the importance of ethical conduct in competitive situations.

"The Five of Swords" serves as a reminder of the multifaceted nature of conflict and the need for ethical consideration in our actions. It encourages navigating disagreements with an awareness of the potential impact on relationships and personal integrity, advocating for resolutions that prioritize mutual respect and understanding.

Six of Swords

"The Six of Swords," a notable card in the Minor Arcana of tarot decks, symbolizes transition, moving on, and the journey towards a more hopeful future. This card is often depicted with a figure steering a boat carrying passengers across a body of water, with swords placed in the vessel, representing the baggage or challenges being carried into the new phase.

Psychologically, The Six of Swords reflects a period of transition and change, moving away from turmoil or difficulty towards a calmer state. It signifies the necessity of leaving behind troubling or difficult situations and advancing towards a more stable and peaceful phase. In readings, this card suggests progression from a challenging period, emphasizing the importance of moving forward, even if the journey is difficult. It encourages the querent to embrace change, understanding that such transitions are necessary for growth and improvement. The Six of Swords resonates with the Jungian concept of individuation, symbolizing the journey of the self from the known to the unknown in the pursuit of psychological wholeness.

The presence of The Six of Swords in a spread indicates a shift away from strife towards a more tranquil environment. It urges the querent to accept the process of change and to understand that while the journey might be challenging, it leads to a more positive destination.

When reversed, The Six of Swords may suggest resistance to change, stagnation, or a journey that is more challenging than anticipated. It might indicate the need to reassess one's path or to find a more effective way to navigate through the current transitions.

"The Six of Swords" thus represents the necessary process of moving on and the journey towards healing and betterment. It personifies the act of leaving behind troubled waters and steering towards a more peaceful future, emphasizing the importance of resilience and adaptability in times of change. The card encourages a forward-looking perspective, recognizing that while transitions can be difficult, they are essential for personal growth and the achievement of a more harmonious state.

Transition and Change: The Six of Swords underscores the theme of transition, highlighting the journey from a difficult phase to a more peaceful and stable one.

Moving On from Turmoil: The card emphasizes the necessity of moving on from turmoil, suggesting the importance of leaving behind challenging situations to embrace new opportunities.

Journey Towards Peace: The Six of Swords is often associated with the journey towards a calmer, more peaceful state, inviting acceptance of change as a part of growth.

Adaptability in Difficult Journeys: The card suggests the need for adaptability and resilience in the face of challenging transitions, encouraging a forward-thinking approach.

Challenges in Reversal: When reversed, The Six of Swords can indicate difficulties in the process of transition, suggesting the need to reassess the approach to change and to seek more effective coping strategies.

The Six of Swords in Personal Development: In the context of personal development, The Six of Swords symbolizes the journey of moving beyond past difficulties towards psychological growth and healing.

"The Six of Swords" serves as a reminder of the inevitability and necessity of change in life's journey. It encourages embracing transitions with resilience and hope, understanding that moving on from the past, though challenging, is essential for finding peace and achieving personal growth.

Seven of Swords

"The Seven of Swords," a thought-provoking card in the Minor Arcana of tarot decks, often represents deception, strategy, and the need to act tactically. This card typically depicts a figure stealthily carrying away swords, suggesting a scenario of secret plans, cunning actions, or avoidance of direct confrontation.

Psychologically, The Seven of Swords indicates a mindset oriented towards indirect strategies or avoidance of direct conflict. It signifies situations where subtlety, cunning, or strategic thinking are employed, often to navigate tricky situations. In readings, this card suggests a time where direct action may not be the most effective approach, encouraging the querent to think strategically and consider alternative methods to achieve their goals. It highlights the complexities of interactions where not everything is as it seems, and where understanding hidden motives and agendas is crucial. The Seven of Swords resonates with the Jungian concept of the trickster, a figure who uses wit and guile to outmaneuver opponents and navigate complex social landscapes.

The presence of The Seven of Swords in a spread calls for a careful reassessment of the situation at hand. It suggests the importance of being aware of deceit or subterfuge, either from others or within oneself. The card urges caution in trust and communication, advising a more guarded approach to interactions.

When reversed, The Seven of Swords may suggest the consequences of deceptive actions, a return to honesty, or the unraveling of a strategy. It might indicate the need to confront issues more directly or to rectify situations where dishonesty or avoidance has played a role.

"The Seven of Swords" thus symbolizes the intricate dance of strategy, caution, and cunning. It personifies the use of intellect and subtlety in complex situations, emphasizing the importance of careful planning and consideration of alternative methods. The card encourages a nuanced approach to challenges, advocating for awareness and strategic thinking in dealings with others and in navigating life's more complicated scenarios.

Strategy and Caution: The Seven of Swords underscores the importance of strategy and caution in dealings. It encourages thinking carefully about actions and considering the implications of various approaches.

Deception and Subtlety: The card emphasizes the themes of deception and subtlety. It suggests being mindful of dishonesty and hidden motives, both in oneself and in others.

Alternative Approaches: The Seven of Swords is often associated with finding alternative solutions to problems. It invites considering non-traditional or indirect methods to achieve goals.

Awareness of Motives: The card suggests the importance of being aware of underlying motives and agendas in interactions, advocating for a more guarded and discerning approach.

Reversal Implications: When reversed, The Seven of Swords can indicate the unraveling of deceitful strategies or a shift towards more direct and honest dealings.

The Seven of Swords in Personal Development: In the context of personal development, The Seven of Swords symbolizes the journey of understanding the complexities of human interaction and the value of strategic thinking and honesty.

"The Seven of Swords" serves as a reminder of the multifaceted nature of human interactions and the importance of strategic awareness. It encourages a thoughtful and cautious approach to complex situations, highlighting the need for discernment, subtlety, and a keen understanding of the dynamics at play.

Eight of Swords

"The Eight of Swords," a compelling card in the Minor Arcana of tarot decks, often symbolizes restriction, self-imposed limitations, and a feeling of entrapment. The card typically depicts a figure blindfolded and bound, surrounded by swords that seem to create a barrier, suggesting a scenario of confinement or powerlessness.

Psychologically, The Eight of Swords represents a state of mind where one feels trapped or restricted, often by their own thoughts or beliefs. It signifies the internal barriers that prevent individuals from moving forward, highlighting the impact of mental constraints on personal freedom. In readings, this card suggests a period where the querent might feel stuck or powerless, encouraging them to recognize that their limitations may be self-imposed. It prompts a reevaluation of one's mindset and challenges the individual to find ways to free themselves from the shackles of their own making. The Eight of Swords resonates with the Jungian concept of the shadow, where fears and unresolved inner conflicts can manifest as external obstacles.

The presence of The Eight of Swords in a spread is an indication to confront the feelings of restriction and to understand that the power to break free lies within. It urges the querent to critically examine their beliefs and perceptions that may be limiting their potential and to seek mental clarity.

When reversed, The Eight of Swords may suggest the beginning of liberation from self-imposed boundaries, or it might point to a continued struggle with finding a way out of a limiting situation. It can indicate that the querent is starting to see the possibilities for change and is seeking ways to overcome the constraints they have imposed on themselves.

"The Eight of Swords" thus embodies the challenge of overcoming mental restrictions and the journey towards self-liberation. It personifies the struggle against internal barriers, emphasizing the importance of self-awareness and mental strength in breaking free from the constraints of fear and self-doubt. The card encourages introspection and a reassessment of one's self-imposed limits, advocating for the power of the mind to overcome challenges and to create new paths towards freedom and empowerment.

Restriction and Limitation: The Eight of Swords highlights the themes of restriction and limitation, particularly those that are self-imposed, encouraging a review of the mental barriers that confine.

Feeling of Entrapment: The card underscores a feeling of entrapment or powerlessness, suggesting that these feelings often stem from internal sources rather than external circumstances.

Breaking Free from Constraints: The Eight of Swords is often associated with the challenge of breaking free from mental constraints and fears, advocating for a shift in perspective to overcome these barriers.

Self-Awareness and Liberation: The card suggests the importance of self-awareness in the process of liberation, emphasizing the need to understand and confront the sources of one's limitations.

Potential for Change: When reversed, The Eight of Swords can signal the beginning of understanding and moving past self-imposed barriers, indicating a shift towards personal empowerment and freedom.

The Eight of Swords in Personal Development: In the context of personal development, The Eight of Swords symbolizes the journey of recognizing and overcoming self-imposed limitations, highlighting the transformative power of self-awareness and mental resilience.

"The Eight of Swords" serves as a powerful reminder of the impact of mental barriers on personal freedom. It encourages a deep dive into the psyche to confront and overcome the fears and beliefs that limit, advocating for the use of inner strength and clarity to break free from the confines of self-imposed restrictions and to embrace the potential for growth and empowerment.

Nine of Swords

"The Nine of Swords," a card in the Minor Arcana of tarot decks, is often associated with anxiety, worry, and the weight of mental anguish. This card typically portrays a figure sitting up in bed, head in hands, as if waking from a nightmare, with nine swords hanging on the wall behind. The imagery conveys a sense of being overwhelmed by one's thoughts or fears, highlighting the struggles of the mind.

Psychologically, The Nine of Swords symbolizes the internal battles with worry, guilt, and despair. It represents the moments when fears and anxieties take hold, often magnified in the stillness of the night. In readings, this card suggests a period where the querent might be experiencing intense worry or mental turmoil, urging them to address the sources of their distress. It highlights the importance of confronting these negative thoughts and seeking support or solutions. The Nine of Swords resonates with the Jungian concept of the 'dark night of the soul', where an individual faces deep psychological challenges, leading to a potential transformation and awakening.

The presence of The Nine of Swords in a spread calls attention to the impact of mental stress and anxiety. It urges the querent to acknowledge their worries and to seek ways to manage and alleviate their mental distress.

When reversed, The Nine of Swords may suggest the beginning of recovery from anxiety, a lessening of worry, or the need to confront unresolved issues that are causing mental strain. It can indicate a shift from a state of despair to one of hope, as the querent starts to see pathways out of their mental anguish.

"The Nine of Swords" thus embodies the struggle with inner fears and anxieties. It personifies the challenges of confronting one's deepest worries, emphasizing the importance of mental health and the need for compassionate self-care. The card encourages an honest assessment of one's mental state, advocating for seeking help and adopting strategies to cope with and overcome anxiety and fear.

Mental Anguish and Worry: The Nine of Swords underscores the themes of mental anguish and worry, highlighting the heavy toll that anxiety and fear can take on the mind.

Confronting Negative Thoughts: The card emphasizes the importance of confronting negative thoughts and fears, suggesting that acknowledging and addressing these concerns is crucial for mental well-being.

Importance of Support: The Nine of Swords is often associated with the need for support and guidance in times of mental distress, inviting the querent to seek help and to talk about their worries.

Shift Towards Recovery: When reversed, The Nine of Swords can signal a movement towards recovery, indicating that the querent is finding ways to manage their anxieties and fears.

The Nine of Swords in Personal Development: In the context of personal development, The Nine of Swords symbolizes the journey of overcoming anxiety and fear, highlighting the importance of mental resilience and the pursuit of inner peace.

"The Nine of Swords" serves as a poignant reminder of the struggles of the human mind. It encourages facing one's fears and anxieties with courage and seeking the support needed to navigate through periods of mental turmoil, emphasizing the power of resilience and hope in the journey towards psychological healing and peace.

Ten of Swords

"The Ten of Swords," a card in the Minor Arcana of tarot decks, is often associated with defeat, betrayal, and the end of a cycle. This card typically features a dramatic image of a figure lying face down, with ten swords in their back, symbolizing a significant and painful conclusion or betrayal.

Psychologically, The Ten of Swords represents the experience of hitting rock bottom, feeling defeated, or suffering a deep betrayal. It signifies moments of profound realization that certain situations or relationships are conclusively over, and it's time to move on. In readings, this card suggests that the querent may be facing a painful ending or a significant loss, urging them to acknowledge this reality and begin the process of healing and moving forward. The Ten of Swords resonates with the Jungian theme of the 'death and rebirth' archetype, where an ending paves the way for new beginnings and personal transformation.

The presence of The Ten of Swords in a spread calls for acceptance of the inevitable and the understanding that from the ashes of defeat, new opportunities can arise. It encourages the querent to let go of what is no longer serving them and to prepare for a new phase in life.

When reversed, The Ten of Swords may suggest that the querent is struggling to accept an ending, or it might indicate that the worst is over, and recovery is on the horizon. It can be a sign that the querent is beginning to see hope and potential for renewal after a period of despair.

"The Ten of Swords" thus symbolizes the challenging but necessary process of confronting painful endings and betrayals. It personifies the acceptance of defeat as a means to closure, emphasizing the importance of resilience and the potential for new beginnings that emerge from difficult situations. The card encourages a perspective that views endings not just as losses, but as essential steps in the cycle of growth and renewal.

Endings and Betrayal: The Ten of Swords underscores the themes of painful endings and betrayal, highlighting the emotional impact of such experiences.

Acceptance of Reality: The card emphasizes the importance of accepting harsh realities, suggesting that acknowledging the end is the first step towards healing and moving forward.

Potential for Renewal: The Ten of Swords is often associated with the potential for renewal that comes after a significant ending, inviting the querent to look towards the future with a renewed perspective.

Resilience in the Face of Defeat: The card suggests resilience in the face of defeat, advocating for a mindset that sees challenges as opportunities for growth and transformation.

Recovery and Hope: When reversed, The Ten of Swords can signal the beginning of recovery from a painful situation, indicating that the querent is finding strength and hope in the aftermath of their struggles.

The Ten of Swords in Personal Development: In the context of personal development, The Ten of Swords symbolizes the journey of learning from difficult endings and using these experiences as catalysts for personal growth and transformation.

"The Ten of Swords" serves as a reminder of the inevitability of endings and the potential for growth that lies in accepting and moving beyond them. It encourages embracing the lessons learned from difficult experiences, understanding that each ending is a precursor to new beginnings and opportunities for personal development.

Page of Swords

"The Page of Swords," a card in the Minor Arcana of tarot decks, typically symbolizes curiosity, mental agility, and a thirst for knowledge. Often depicted is a youthful figure standing in a breezy landscape, holding a sword upright. This image conveys a sense of readiness, alertness, and eagerness to engage with the world of ideas and communication.

Psychologically, The Page of Swords represents the lively aspect of the mind that is always seeking, questioning, and exploring new ideas and perspectives. It signifies intellectual curiosity, a desire to learn, and the early stages of intellectual or communicative endeavors. In readings, this card suggests a period where the querent might be exploring new ways of thinking, gathering information, or expressing themselves. It encourages a proactive approach to learning and communication, highlighting the importance of staying open and adaptable. The Page of Swords resonates with the Jungian archetype of the puer aeternus or eternal youth, embodying the spirit of exploration, discovery, and the endless pursuit of knowledge.

The presence of The Page of Swords in a spread indicates a time of intellectual growth and the exploration of new ideas. It urges the querent to embrace their curiosity, to ask questions, and to engage with the world with an open and inquisitive mind.

When reversed, The Page of Swords may suggest hasty thinking, miscommunication, or using one's intellect in a superficial or deceptive manner. It might indicate the need to slow down, to think things through more carefully, or to be more sincere in communication.

"The Page of Swords" thus represents the dynamic energy of the mind that is always ready to learn and communicate. It personifies the youthful vigor of intellectual pursuits, emphasizing the importance of curiosity, open-mindedness, and the desire for understanding. The card encourages an enthusiastic approach to learning and communication, advocating for the exploration of new ideas and the expression of one's thoughts with clarity and honesty.

Intellectual Curiosity and Exploration: The Page of Swords underscores the importance of intellectual curiosity and the exploration of new ideas. It encourages an inquisitive and open-minded approach to learning.

Engagement with Ideas and Communication: The card emphasizes engagement with the world of ideas and effective communication. It invites the querent to express themselves clearly and to seek understanding in conversations.

Youthful Enthusiasm and Discovery: The Page of Swords is often associated with the energy and enthusiasm of youth in intellectual pursuits, suggesting a period of discovery and growth.

Awareness in Communication: The card suggests the importance of being aware and thoughtful in communication, avoiding hasty or superficial conversations.

Potential Miscommunication: When reversed, The Page of Swords can indicate challenges in communication, such as misunderstandings or misuse of words, urging a more careful and deliberate approach.

The Page of Swords in Personal Development: In the context of personal development, The Page of Swords symbolizes the journey of intellectual growth and the development of effective communication skills.

"The Page of Swords" serves as a reminder of the vitality and potential of the young mind. It encourages embracing the journey of learning and communication, highlighting the value of curiosity, open-mindedness, and a sincere desire to understand and engage with the world around us.

Knight of Swords

"The Knight of Swords," a dynamic card in the Minor Arcana of tarot decks, often represents boldness, ambition, and a strong-willed pursuit of goals. This card typically features a knight in armor, charging forward on a powerful steed, sword drawn and ready for battle. The image conveys a sense of swift action, determination, and the courage to face challenges head-on.

Psychologically, The Knight of Swords symbolizes the aspect of the mind that is assertive, driven, and eager to confront obstacles. It signifies a period of intense focus on goals, a willingness to tackle intellectual challenges, and a propensity for decisive action. In readings, this card suggests a time where the querent is or needs to be assertive in their pursuits, encouraging them to take bold steps and to speak their truth without hesitation. The Knight of Swords resonates with the Jungian archetype of the hero on a quest, embodying the qualities of bravery, directness, and a spirited approach to problem-solving.

The presence of The Knight of Swords in a spread indicates a phase of proactive engagement with the world, marked by a rapid advancement towards goals. It urges the querent to harness their mental energy, to think and act swiftly, and to embrace the challenges that lie ahead with confidence.

When reversed, The Knight of Swords may suggest recklessness, impulsive actions, or a lack of forethought. It might indicate the need to temper one's drive with consideration and to avoid rushing into situations without adequate planning.

"The Knight of Swords" thus embodies the vigorous pursuit of intellectual and communicative endeavors. It personifies the qualities of assertiveness and determination in the face of challenges, emphasizing the importance of clarity of thought and purposeful action. The card encourages a bold and direct approach to achieving objectives, advocating for the use of intellect and communication as tools to navigate and overcome obstacles.

Boldness and Ambition: The Knight of Swords underscores the qualities of boldness and ambition, highlighting the drive to pursue goals with determination and confidence.

Swift Action and Determination: The card emphasizes swift action and a strong will to confront challenges, inviting the querent to take decisive steps towards their objectives.

Heroic Quest and Problem-Solving: The Knight of Swords is often associated with the heroic quest, representing a spirited and direct approach to problem-solving and goal achievement.

Balancing Drive with Consideration: The card suggests the importance of balancing one's ambitious drive with careful consideration, avoiding impulsive actions that may lead to unintended consequences.

Reversed Implications: When reversed, The Knight of Swords can indicate a tendency towards recklessness or haste, urging a more thoughtful and measured approach to pursuits.

The Knight of Swords in Personal Development: In the context of personal development, The Knight of Swords symbolizes the journey of harnessing one's mental energy and assertiveness, fostering a proactive and courageous approach to life's challenges.

"The Knight of Swords" serves as a reminder of the power of directed ambition and the value of assertive action. It encourages embracing the qualities of bravery and determination in the pursuit of goals, highlighting the effectiveness of a bold and forthright approach in overcoming obstacles and achieving success.

Queen of Swords

"The Queen of Swords," a card in the Minor Arcana of tarot decks, represents clarity of thought, intellectual power, and independence. This card typically features a regal figure, often seated on a throne, holding a straight sword pointing upward. The queen's demeanor is one of calm authority, symbolizing a mind that is sharp, clear, and unbiased.

Psychologically, The Queen of Swords signifies a mastery of intellect and communication. She embodies wisdom, honesty, and an ability to see through deception and falsehood. This card suggests a person who relies on logic and understanding, often indicating a time for making decisions based on clear thinking and direct communication. In readings, this card encourages the querent to embrace honesty, to communicate clearly, and to rely on their intellect and perception. The Queen of Swords resonates with the Jungian archetype of the wise woman, representing the integration of intelligence and experience in decision-making and problem-solving.

The presence of The Queen of Swords in a spread signals a period where intellect and clear communication are paramount. It urges the querent to approach situations with honesty and directness, to think critically, and to speak their truth with confidence.

When reversed, The Queen of Swords may suggest coldness, bitterness, or a too-critical nature. It might indicate the need to temper intellect with empathy, to be mindful of how one's words and thoughts affect others.

"The Queen of Swords" thus embodies the qualities of intellectual clarity and straightforward communication. It personifies the wise use of mental acuity, emphasizing the importance of honesty, clear thinking, and the ability to cut through confusion and ambiguity. The card encourages a balanced approach to communication, combining wisdom with directness, and advocating for the use of intellect as a tool for understanding and navigating the complexities of life.

Intellectual Clarity and Honesty: The Queen of Swords underscores the importance of intellectual clarity and honesty, highlighting the value of clear thinking and straightforward communication.

Mastery of Intellect and Perception: The card emphasizes the mastery of intellect and the ability to see through deception, inviting the querent to rely on their intelligence and insight.

Wise Decision-Making: The Queen of Swords is often associated with wise decision-making, representing the integration of experience and intellect in navigating life's challenges.

Balancing Logic with Empathy: The card suggests the need to balance logic and critical thinking with empathy and understanding, ensuring that communication is both clear and considerate.

Reversed Implications: When reversed, The Queen of Swords can indicate an overly critical or emotionally detached approach, urging a more balanced and empathetic perspective.

The Queen of Swords in Personal Development: In the context of personal development, The Queen of Swords symbolizes the journey of developing intellectual strength and clear communication skills, fostering a wise and balanced approach to life's situations.

"The Queen of Swords" serves as a reminder of the power of the intellect and the value of clear, honest communication. It encourages embracing intellectual strength and clarity, advocating for a wise and straightforward approach in expressing oneself and making decisions.

King of Swords

"The King of Swords," a card in the Minor Arcana of tarot decks, epitomizes the embodiment of intellectual authority, strategic leadership, and ethical judgment. This card typically portrays a stern, commanding figure seated on a throne, holding an upright sword, representing the power of intellect and reason in leadership.

Psychologically, The King of Swords represents the aspect of the mind that is analytical, authoritative, and fair. He signifies clear thinking, the ability to make decisions based on reason and justice, and the capacity to see the truth in complex situations. In readings, this card suggests a time where the querent might need to embody or seek guidance from someone who possesses these qualities. It encourages making decisions based on careful thought and moral principles, emphasizing the importance of intellectual leadership and ethical integrity. The King of Swords resonates with the Jungian archetype of the wise king or judge, symbolizing the mature integration of intellect and ethics in decision-making.

The presence of The King of Swords in a spread calls for a rational and balanced approach to problem-solving. It suggests the importance of being objective, using one's intellect to navigate through challenges, and ensuring decisions are made with fairness and integrity.

When reversed, The King of Swords may suggest a misuse of intellectual power, a lack of fairness, or an overly critical or cold approach. It might indicate the need for the querent to review their decision-making process, to ensure they are not being unfair or overly analytical at the expense of empathy.

"The King of Swords" thus symbolizes the ideal of intellectual mastery and ethical leadership. It personifies the qualities of clarity of thought, strategic planning, and moral responsibility, emphasizing the importance of using one's intellect and ethical understanding to guide actions and decisions. The card encourages a leadership style that values truth, justice, and rationality, advocating for the responsible use of intellectual power in both personal and public spheres.

Intellectual Authority and Clarity: The King of Swords underscores the importance of intellectual authority and clarity of thought, highlighting the value of reasoned judgment and clear decision-making.

Ethical Leadership and Fairness: The card emphasizes ethical leadership and the need for fairness in judgments, inviting the querent to consider the moral implications of their decisions.

Strategic Planning and Decision-Making: The King of Swords is often associated with strategic planning and effective decision-making, suggesting a careful and balanced approach to problem-solving.

Rationality and Objectivity: The card suggests the importance of rationality and objectivity, advocating for a thoughtful and unbiased approach to challenges.

Reversed Implications: When reversed, The King of Swords can indicate potential issues with the use of intellectual power, such as unfairness or a lack of empathy, urging a more balanced and compassionate approach.

The King of Swords in Personal Development: In the context of personal development, The King of Swords symbolizes the journey of developing intellectual strength and ethical responsibility, fostering a mature and wise approach to leadership and decision-making.

"The King of Swords" serves as a reminder of the power of an analytical and ethical mind. It encourages embracing intellectual leadership and fairness, highlighting the effectiveness of a rational, moral approach in navigating life's complexities and guiding others.

The Wands Series

The Ace of Wands

"The Ace of Wands," a card in the Minor Arcana of tarot decks, is a symbol of inspiration, new beginnings, and creative energy. This card typically depicts a hand emerging from a cloud, holding a flourishing wand, signifying the spark of new ideas, the birth of enthusiasm, and the initiation of action.

Psychologically, The Ace of Wands represents a surge of creative power and the excitement of embarking on new ventures. It signifies moments of sudden inspiration and the urge to start new projects or express oneself creatively. In readings, this card suggests a period ripe for pursuing new ideas, embracing creative impulses, and taking the initiative. It encourages the querent to act on their passions and to harness their creative energies to bring about change and growth. The Ace of Wands resonates with the Jungian concept of the creative self, embodying the potential for self-expression and the realization of one's creative ambitions.

The presence of The Ace of Wands in a spread indicates a time of great potential and enthusiasm. It urges the querent to seize the moment, to be bold in their pursuits, and to let their creative spirit lead the way.

When reversed, The Ace of Wands may suggest a delay in the onset of new ventures, a lack of motivation, or a block in creative energy. It might indicate the need to reignite one's passion, to find inspiration, or to reassess the direction of one's creative efforts.

"The Ace of Wands" thus symbolizes the awakening of creative power and the excitement of new beginnings. It personifies the initial spark that ignites passion and the desire to create, emphasizing the importance of enthusiasm, innovation, and the courage to take the first steps in a new direction. The card encourages embracing the creative process, advocating for the transformational power of original ideas and the pursuit of one's passions with zeal and vigor.

Creative Energy and Inspiration: The Ace of Wands underscores the importance of creative energy and inspiration, highlighting the potential for innovation and the birth of new ideas.

Initiative and New Ventures: The card emphasizes the value of taking the initiative in pursuing new ventures, inviting the querent to act on their impulses and to start new projects.

The Spark of Enthusiasm: The Ace of Wands is often associated with the spark of enthusiasm and the excitement of beginning something new, suggesting a period of heightened creative and entrepreneurial spirit.

Reversal Implications: When reversed, The Ace of Wands can indicate challenges in harnessing creative energy, such as delays or blocks, urging a rekindling of passion and inspiration.

The Ace of Wands in Personal Development: In the context of personal development, The Ace of Wands symbolizes the journey of embracing one's creative potential and the power of originality in personal expression.

"The Ace of Wands" serves as a reminder of the transformative power of creativity and the importance of embracing new beginnings with excitement and confidence. It encourages tapping into one's creative spirit, using it as a force for growth, innovation, and the expression of one's unique perspective.

Two of Wands

"The Two of Wands," a card in the Minor Arcana of tarot decks, symbolizes planning, decision-making, and the potential for future progress. This card often depicts a figure holding a globe in one hand and a wand in the other, standing on a battlement and looking out over a vast landscape. The imagery conveys a sense of foresight, contemplation, and the weighing of options for the future.

Psychologically, The Two of Wands represents the phase of considering one's path forward, having already taken the initial steps towards a goal. It signifies the moment of contemplating potential actions and outcomes, symbolizing the mental process of planning and strategizing. In readings, this card suggests a time where the querent is or should be considering their future direction, urging them to make thoughtful choices and to expand their horizons. It encourages proactive planning and the exploration of possibilities beyond the familiar. The Two of Wands resonates with the Jungian concept of individuation, where one seeks to realize their unique potential through conscious decision-making and self-reflection.

The presence of The Two of Wands in a spread indicates a period of opportunity and potential. It urges the querent to embrace strategic thinking, to consider their long-term goals, and to be bold in charting their course.

When reversed, The Two of Wands may suggest fear of the unknown, hesitation in decision-making, or a lack of direction. It might indicate the need to overcome self-imposed barriers or to reevaluate one's plans to find a clearer path forward.

"The Two of Wands" thus symbolizes the journey of exploring possibilities and making decisions that shape one's future. It personifies the process of strategic planning and foresight, emphasizing the importance of thoughtful consideration in the pursuit of goals. The card encourages embracing the potential for growth and expansion, advocating for a proactive approach in shaping one's destiny.

Planning and Decision-Making: The Two of Wands underscores the importance of planning and decision-making, highlighting the need for foresight and strategic thinking in shaping one's future.

Exploration of Possibilities: The card emphasizes the exploration of possibilities and the consideration of different paths, inviting the querent to expand their horizons and think beyond their current circumstances.

Strategic Foresight: The Two of Wands is often associated with strategic foresight, representing the thoughtful contemplation of future actions and goals.

Overcoming Hesitation: When reversed, The Two of Wands can indicate challenges in decision-making, such as hesitation or fear of the unknown, urging a more confident and determined approach.

The Two of Wands in Personal Development: In the context of personal development, The Two of Wands symbolizes the journey of realizing one's potential through conscious planning and the exploration of new opportunities.

"The Two of Wands" serves as a reminder of the power of thoughtful planning and the value of considering one's future direction. It encourages embracing the process of decision-making with an open and strategic mind, recognizing the potential that lies in carefully charting one's path towards growth and fulfillment.

Three of Wands

"The Three of Wands," a card in the Minor Arcana of tarot decks, symbolizes foresight, expansion, and looking towards the future with optimism. This card often depicts a figure standing on a high vantage point, gazing out over a vast landscape or sea, with three wands firmly planted around them. The imagery suggests a sense of anticipation and readiness for the opportunities that are emerging.

Psychologically, The Three of Wands represents the mindset of looking forward and preparing for what is to come. It signifies a phase of growth and expansion, where past efforts begin to bear fruit, and the potential for new ventures is realized. In readings, this card suggests a period of progress and forward movement, encouraging the querent to continue building on their plans and to remain open to new opportunities. It highlights the importance of strategic planning and a broad vision for the future. The Three of Wands resonates with the Jungian concept of individuation, where an individual steps beyond the known boundaries to embrace growth and self-realization.

The presence of The Three of Wands in a spread indicates a time of potential and anticipation. It urges the querent to maintain their course, to stay committed to their goals, and to be ready to seize new opportunities that arise.

When reversed, The Three of Wands may suggest delays, obstacles, or a reassessment of future plans. It might indicate the need to adjust one's approach or to cultivate patience as plans unfold.

"The Three of Wands" thus symbolizes the journey of looking ahead with hope and expectation. It personifies the readiness to embrace new challenges and opportunities, emphasizing the importance of a forward-thinking attitude and the willingness to venture into new territories. The card encourages an optimistic outlook, advocating for the value of perseverance, strategic planning, and the pursuit of expansion and growth.

Vision and Expansion: The Three of Wands underscores the themes of vision and expansion, highlighting the need for foresight and strategic planning in pursuing one's goals.

Preparation for Future Opportunities: The card emphasizes the importance of being prepared for future opportunities, suggesting an openness to new possibilities and a readiness to embrace change.

Progress and Forward Movement: The Three of Wands is often associated with progress and forward movement, representing the phase of growth where one's efforts begin to show results.

Adaptability and Patience: When reversed, The Three of Wands can indicate a need for adaptability and patience, suggesting adjustments in plans or strategies in response to changing circumstances.

The Three of Wands in Personal Development: In the context of personal development, The Three of Wands symbolizes the journey of expanding one's horizons and embracing growth, fostering a mindset of optimism and readiness for new challenges.

"The Three of Wands" serves as a reminder of the power of forward-thinking and the potential that lies in embracing new opportunities. It encourages maintaining a vision for the future, staying committed to one's path, and being open to the possibilities that arise, highlighting the importance of growth, expansion, and optimistic anticipation in the journey of life.

Four of Wands

"The Four of Wands," a card in the Minor Arcana of tarot decks, symbolizes celebration, harmony, and a sense of achievement and stability. This card is often depicted with four wands standing in the foreground, framing a festive scene, sometimes with figures joyously celebrating, symbolizing a time of well-deserved success and communal harmony.

Psychologically, The Four of Wands represents the feeling of satisfaction that comes from achieving a significant milestone or goal.

It signifies a period of stability and joy, where one's efforts have led to a harmonious and rewarding outcome. In readings, this card suggests a time of celebration, urging the querent to acknowledge their achievements and to share their joy with others. It encourages recognizing the importance of community and support in one's success and highlights the value of creating a stable and harmonious environment. The Four of Wands resonates with the Jungian concept of the collective unconscious, emphasizing the shared human experience of celebration and the communal aspect of achievement.

The presence of The Four of Wands in a spread indicates a phase of fulfillment and communal joy. It urges the querent to enjoy the fruits of their labor, to celebrate their achievements, and to embrace the stability and harmony they have created.

When reversed, The Four of Wands may suggest a delay in celebration, a lack of harmony, or challenges in achieving a sense of stability. It might indicate the need to work on creating balance in one's life or to address issues that are preventing the full enjoyment of success.

"The Four of Wands" thus symbolizes the joy of accomplishment and the importance of communal celebration. It personifies the satisfaction that comes from achieving goals and creating harmony, emphasizing the importance of sharing success with others and the value of a supportive community. The card encourages a spirit of gratitude and celebration, advocating for the recognition of achievements and the creation of a joyful and stable environment.

Celebration and Achievement: The Four of Wands underscores the themes of celebration and achievement, highlighting the joy of reaching significant milestones.

Community and Harmony: The card emphasizes the importance of community and harmony in one's successes, suggesting the value of sharing achievements and creating a supportive environment.

Gratitude and Fulfillment: The Four of Wands is often associated with feelings of gratitude and fulfillment, representing the satisfaction that comes from hard work and the achievement of stability.

Reversed Implications: When reversed, The Four of Wands can indicate challenges in finding joy and harmony, urging a focus on creating balance and addressing issues that hinder celebration.

The Four of Wands in Personal Development: In the context of personal development, The Four of Wands symbolizes the journey of recognizing and celebrating one's achievements, fostering a sense of joy, stability, and communal support.

"The Four of Wands" serves as a reminder of the power of celebration and the importance of community in achieving success. It encourages embracing the joy of accomplishments, sharing this happiness with others, and recognizing the role of communal support in the journey towards personal fulfillment and harmony.

Five of Wands

"The Five of Wands," a card in the Minor Arcana of tarot decks, represents conflict, competition, and the challenges of dealing with opposing viewpoints or interests. This card typically depicts a scene of five individuals, each holding a wand, in a state of apparent conflict or competition, symbolizing a clash of ideas, goals, or desires.

Psychologically, The Five of Wands signifies the internal and external struggles that arise from competing interests or conflicting viewpoints. It represents the challenges of navigating disagreements and the dynamics of group conflicts. In readings, this card suggests a period of strife or competition, encouraging the querent to understand the nature of the conflict and to seek constructive ways to address it. It highlights the importance of learning how to manage disagreements and to use conflict as an opportunity for growth and clarification. The Five of Wands resonates with the Jungian concept of the shadow, where conflicting aspects within oneself or with others can lead to tension and struggle.

The presence of The Five of Wands in a spread indicates a time of challenge and competition. It urges the querent to stay resilient, to understand the root causes of the conflict, and to approach disagreements with a mindset geared toward resolution and understanding.

When reversed, The Five of Wands may suggest a resolution to conflict, a retreat from competition, or the need to reassess one's approach to handling disagreements. It might indicate a period of reflection on how to better manage conflicts or to find harmony in the midst of competition.

"The Five of Wands" thus symbolizes the complexities of conflict and competition. It personifies the challenges of dealing with opposing forces, emphasizing the importance of resilience, strategic thinking, and the pursuit of constructive resolution. The card encourages facing conflicts head-on, advocating for the use of such challenges as opportunities for personal growth, improved communication, and a deeper understanding of different perspectives.

Conflict and Competition: The Five of Wands underscores the themes of conflict and competition, highlighting the challenges of navigating disagreements and the clash of differing viewpoints.

Management of Disagreements: The card emphasizes the importance of managing disagreements constructively, inviting the querent to approach conflicts with the aim of resolution and growth.

Learning from Conflict: The Five of Wands is often associated with the lessons that can be learned from conflict, suggesting that such challenges offer opportunities for clarification and personal development.

Reversed Implications: When reversed, The Five of Wands can indicate a move towards resolution or a reassessment of how to handle conflicts, urging a more harmonious approach to managing disagreements.

The Five of Wands in Personal Development: In the context of personal development, The Five of Wands symbolizes the journey of understanding the dynamics of conflict and using these experiences as catalysts for growth and improved communication.

"The Five of Wands" serves as a reminder of the inevitable presence of conflict in human interactions. It encourages embracing the challenges of competition and disagreement as pathways to better understanding, effective communication, and personal growth, highlighting the value of resilience and strategic thinking in navigating life's conflicts.

Six of Wands

"The Six of Wands," a card in the Minor Arcana of tarot decks, symbolizes success, recognition, and triumph. This card is often depicted with a figure riding victoriously on a horse, with a wand held high, often adorned with a laurel or wreath, symbolizing the achievement of goals and the receiving of accolades or praise.

Psychologically, The Six of Wands represents the feelings of confidence and pride that come from accomplishments and recognition. It signifies moments of personal or professional triumph, where one's efforts are acknowledged and celebrated. In readings, this card suggests a period of success and public acknowledgment, encouraging the querent to embrace and enjoy the recognition they have earned. It highlights the importance of self-confidence and the positive impact of public acclaim. The Six of Wands resonates with the Jungian concept of the victorious hero, embodying the fulfillment and empowerment that come from achieving one's goals.

The presence of The Six of Wands in a spread indicates a time of achievement and recognition. It urges the querent to acknowledge their successes and to enjoy the rewards of their hard work, while also remaining humble and grateful.

When reversed, The Six of Wands may suggest a delay in recognition, a lack of acknowledgment, or the presence of false pride. It might indicate the need to reassess one's pursuit of acclaim or to consider the more intrinsic aspects of success beyond public recognition.

"The Six of Wands" thus symbolizes the joy and fulfillment that come from achievement and recognition. It personifies the triumph of overcoming challenges and the validation that comes from external acknowledgment, emphasizing the importance of self-confidence and the positive reinforcement of success. The card encourages a balanced approach to success, advocating for the appreciation of both external accolades and internal satisfaction in one's accomplishments.

Success and Recognition: The Six of Wands underscores the themes of success and recognition, highlighting the joys of achievement and the positive impact of public acclaim.

Confidence and Pride: The card emphasizes the importance of confidence and pride in one's accomplishments, inviting the querent to celebrate their victories and enjoy their moment of triumph.

The Six of Wands is often associated with public acclaim and acknowledgment, representing the external validation of one's efforts and achievements.

Reversed Implications: When reversed, The Six of Wands can indicate challenges in receiving recognition, suggesting a need to focus on intrinsic rewards and personal fulfillment.

The Six of Wands in Personal Development: In the context of personal development, The Six of Wands symbolizes the journey of achieving one's goals and the fulfillment that comes from external and internal validation.

"The Six of Wands" serves as a reminder of the rewards of hard work and the importance of recognizing one's achievements. It encourages embracing the moments of triumph, valuing both the public recognition and the personal satisfaction that come from success, and maintaining a balanced perspective on achievement and acclaim.

Seven of Wands

"The Seven of Wands," a card in the Minor Arcana of tarot decks, represents determination, defense, and standing one's ground in the face of challenges. This card typically depicts a figure standing on higher ground, wielding a wand in defense against six other wands that are raised towards them from below, symbolizing a stance of resilience and assertiveness in the face of opposition.

Psychologically, The Seven of Wands signifies the inner strength and resolve needed to confront and overcome challenges or opposition. It represents the courage to maintain one's position and to defend one's beliefs or achievements against adversaries. In readings, this card suggests a period where the querent might be facing opposition or competition, urging them to stay determined and to defend their stance. It highlights the importance of self-belief and the need to assert oneself in challenging situations. The Seven of Wands resonates with the Jungian archetype of the warrior, embodying the qualities of courage, perseverance, and the struggle to uphold one's principles.

The presence of The Seven of Wands in a spread indicates a time of standing firm against challenges. It urges the querent to trust in their own strength and convictions, to remain steadfast, and to confront any opposition with confidence and determination.

When reversed, The Seven of Wands may suggest feeling overwhelmed by challenges, a retreat from opposition, or the need to reassess one's position. It might indicate the need to adopt a more flexible approach or to consider whether the battle at hand is worth the effort.

"The Seven of Wands" thus symbolizes the challenge of defending one's position and the importance of resilience in the face of adversity. It personifies the struggle to maintain one's ground and to confront challenges head-on, emphasizing the importance of courage, determination, and self-belief. The card encourages standing up for oneself and one's beliefs, advocating for the value of perseverance and assertiveness in overcoming obstacles and upholding one's integrity.

Determination and Defense: The Seven of Wands underscores the themes of determination and defense, highlighting the need to stand one's ground and to confront challenges with resilience.

Courage and Perseverance: The card emphasizes the qualities of courage and perseverance, inviting the querent to maintain their position and to defend their beliefs with conviction.

Confronting Opposition: The Seven of Wands is often associated with confronting opposition or competition, representing the struggle to uphold one's principles in the face of adversity.

Flexibility and Reassessment: When reversed, The Seven of Wands can indicate a need for flexibility or a reassessment of one's stance, suggesting a consideration of different approaches to challenges.

The Seven of Wands in Personal Development: In the context of personal development, The Seven of Wands symbolizes the journey of developing inner strength and the ability to assert oneself in challenging situations.

"The Seven of Wands" serves as a reminder of the power of resilience and the importance of standing up for oneself. It encourages embracing the challenges of life with determination and self-belief, recognizing the value of perseverance and assertiveness in defending one's position and maintaining personal integrity.

Eight of Wands

"The Eight of Wands," a card in the Minor Arcana of tarot decks, symbolizes rapid movement, swift change, and the swift unfolding of events. This card is often depicted with eight wands flying through the air, as if in mid-flight, symbolizing speed, progress, and the rapid advancement towards goals.

Psychologically, The Eight of Wands represents the acceleration of thoughts and actions, signifying a period of dynamic progress and rapid movement. It suggests a time when things are moving forward quickly, where plans and ideas begin to manifest with remarkable speed. In readings, this card indicates a phase of rapid development, urging the querent to seize the momentum and to act swiftly. It highlights the importance of aligning one's actions with the fast-paced changes and taking advantage of the current flow of energy. The Eight of Wands resonates with the Jungian archetype of the pathfinder or explorer, embodying the journey of swiftly navigating through life's challenges and opportunities.

The presence of The Eight of Wands in a spread suggests that events are moving at a fast pace, encouraging the querent to keep up with the changes and to act decisively. It is a call to embrace the swift unfolding of events and to use the momentum to one's advantage.

When reversed, The Eight of Wands may suggest delays, slow progress, or obstacles in the path of rapid development. It might indicate the need to reassess one's approach or to find ways to overcome the hurdles that are slowing down progress.

"The Eight of Wands" thus symbolizes the rapid flow of energy and the acceleration of action. It personifies the swift advancement towards goals and the exhilaration of rapid progress, emphasizing the importance of quick thinking and adaptability. The card encourages embracing the pace of change, advocating for the effective use of momentum in pursuing ambitions and realizing plans.

Rapid Movement and Swift Change: The Eight of Wands underscores the themes of rapid movement and swift change, highlighting the dynamic nature of progress and advancement.

Seizing Momentum: The card emphasizes the importance of seizing the momentum, inviting the querent to act swiftly and to align with the pace of unfolding events.

Adaptability and Quick Thinking: The Eight of Wands is often associated with adaptability and quick thinking, representing the need to swiftly navigate through changes and opportunities.

Challenges in Reversal: When reversed, The Eight of Wands can indicate challenges in maintaining the pace, suggesting a need to address delays or obstacles that hinder progress.

The Eight of Wands in Personal Development: In the context of personal development, The Eight of Wands symbolizes the journey of embracing rapid change and using it as a catalyst for swift advancement and achievement.

"The Eight of Wands" serves as a reminder of the power of momentum and the importance of keeping pace with life's rapid changes. It encourages embracing the swift flow of events, utilizing quick thinking and adaptability to turn opportunities into achievements, and moving confidently towards one's goals.

Nine of Wands

"The Nine of Wands," a card in the Minor Arcana of tarot decks, symbolizes resilience, persistence, and the readiness to face challenges. This card often depicts a figure standing guard, wounded but steadfast, with nine wands positioned as a protective barrier, conveying a sense of vigilance and preparedness after enduring hardships.

Psychologically, The Nine of Wands represents the inner strength and determination required to persevere through difficulties. It signifies a state of cautious readiness, having faced trials and being prepared for what may come next. In readings, this card suggests a period of resilience and endurance, encouraging the querent to stay strong and to keep their defenses up. It highlights the importance of learning from past experiences and using that knowledge to fortify oneself against future challenges. The Nine of Wands resonates with the Jungian archetype of the survivor, embodying the qualities of endurance, vigilance, and the protective instincts developed through overcoming adversity.

The presence of The Nine of Wands in a spread indicates a phase of fortitude and guarded readiness. It urges the querent to draw upon their resilience, to remain vigilant, and to prepare for any further challenges while preserving their hard-won gains.

When reversed, The Nine of Wands may suggest exhaustion from constant vigilance, a feeling of being overwhelmed, or the need to let down one's guard. It might indicate the need to reassess one's defensive stance or to find a balance between caution and openness.

"The Nine of Wands" thus symbolizes the challenge of maintaining resilience in the face of ongoing adversity. It personifies the struggle to protect one's achievements and the importance of staying alert and prepared. The card encourages a balance between guarding against potential threats and recognizing when it is safe to relax one's defenses, advocating for the value of endurance, learning from the past, and the wise management of one's resources and strengths.

Resilience and Persistence: The Nine of Wands underscores the themes of resilience and persistence, highlighting the need for steadfastness and endurance through challenges.

Vigilance and Preparedness: The card emphasizes vigilance and preparedness, inviting the querent to stay alert and ready to face potential challenges.

Learning from Experience: The Nine of Wands is often associated with the wisdom gained from experience, suggesting the importance of using past trials to strengthen one's position.

Reversed Implications: When reversed, The Nine of Wands can indicate fatigue from constant vigilance or a need to reassess one's defensive stance, urging a more balanced approach to protection and openness.

The Nine of Wands in Personal Development: In the context of personal development, The Nine of Wands symbolizes the journey of developing resilience and the capacity to withstand adversity while remaining vigilant and prepared for future challenges.

"The Nine of Wands" serves as a reminder of the power of endurance and the importance of learning from one's experiences. It encourages embracing the qualities of resilience and preparedness, recognizing the value of vigilance in protecting one's achievements, and finding a balance between defense and openness in the journey of life.

Ten of Wands

"The Ten of Wands," a card in the Minor Arcana of tarot decks, symbolizes the burden of responsibilities, the feeling of being overwhelmed, and the challenges of carrying a heavy load. This card typically depicts a figure struggling to carry ten wands, often bent under their weight, conveying a sense of exertion and overcommitment.

Psychologically, The Ten of Wands represents the mental and emotional strain that comes from taking on too much or trying to manage an excessive burden. It signifies moments when responsibilities become overwhelming, reflecting the need to reassess one's priorities and perhaps delegate or release some duties. In readings, this card suggests a period of significant stress due to overextension, urging the querent to consider ways to lighten their load or to seek help. It highlights the importance of recognizing one's limits and the need for balance between ambition and well-being. The Ten of Wands resonates with the Jungian archetype of the martyr, embodying the struggle and self-sacrifice associated with taking on more than one can comfortably handle.

The presence of The Ten of Wands in a spread indicates a time of burden and the need for reassessment. It urges the querent to acknowledge their limits, to seek support, and to find more sustainable ways of handling their responsibilities.

When reversed, The Ten of Wands may suggest the beginning of a release from burdens, an opportunity to delegate responsibilities, or the realization that it is time to let go of unnecessary obligations. It might indicate the need to reassess one's commitments and to prioritize self-care and personal well-being.

"The Ten of Wands" thus symbolizes the challenge of managing heavy burdens and the importance of acknowledging one's limits. It personifies the struggle of bearing excessive responsibilities, emphasizing the importance of balance, the need for support, and the value of recognizing when to release or redistribute the load. The card encourages seeking a more manageable approach to responsibilities, advocating for the importance of self-care and the judicious management of one's duties and ambitions.

Burden and Overwhelm: The Ten of Wands underscores the themes of burden and feeling overwhelmed, highlighting the challenges of managing excessive responsibilities.

Acknowledging Limits: The card emphasizes the importance of acknowledging one's limits, inviting the querent to reassess their commitments and to seek more sustainable ways of handling tasks.

Need for Support and Balance: The Ten of Wands is often associated with the need for support and finding balance, representing the value of delegation and prioritizing well-being.

Reversed Implications: When reversed, The Ten of Wands can indicate a release from burdens, suggesting a shift towards lighter responsibilities and improved self-care.

The Ten of Wands in Personal Development: In the context of personal development, The Ten of Wands symbolizes the journey of understanding one's capacity and the importance of balancing ambition with personal well-being.

"The Ten of Wands" serves as a reminder of the impact of taking on too much and the importance of self-care in the face of demanding responsibilities. It encourages a thoughtful approach to managing one's duties, recognizing the need for balance, support, and the wisdom in knowing when to lighten the load.

Page of Wands

"The Page of Wands," a card in the Minor Arcana of tarot decks, represents enthusiasm, exploration, and the beginning of a creative journey or adventure. This card often depicts a young, energetic figure holding a wand, gazing at it with curiosity and anticipation, symbolizing the potential for creative expression and the excitement of new beginnings.

Psychologically, The Page of Wands signifies the awakening of one's creative impulses and the desire to express oneself in new and innovative ways. It represents the early stages of creative or intellectual endeavors, filled with potential and enthusiasm. In readings, this card suggests a period of discovery and exploration, encouraging the querent to pursue their interests and passions with an open and eager mindset. It highlights the importance of curiosity and the willingness to embark on new adventures. The Page of Wands resonates with the Jungian archetype of the child, embodying the spirit of exploration, curiosity, and the joy of learning and growing.

The presence of The Page of Wands in a spread indicates a time of opportunity and potential for creative growth. It urges the querent to embrace their curiosity, to explore new ideas, and to approach life with a sense of adventure and openness.

When reversed, The Page of Wands may suggest a lack of direction, unrefined potential, or hesitation to embark on a new journey. It might indicate the need to focus one's energies, to find inspiration, or to develop a clearer sense of purpose.

"The Page of Wands" thus symbolizes the excitement and potential of the early stages of creative and intellectual growth. It personifies the enthusiasm of youth, emphasizing the importance of exploration, curiosity, and the willingness to learn and try new things. The card encourages embracing the journey of discovery, advocating for the value of passion, creativity, and the pursuit of one's interests with energy and optimism.

Enthusiasm and Exploration: The Page of Wands underscores the themes of enthusiasm and exploration, highlighting the excitement of new beginnings and creative expression.

Creative Potential and Curiosity: The card emphasizes the importance of embracing creative potential and maintaining curiosity, inviting the querent to pursue their passions and interests.

Spirit of Adventure: The Page of Wands is often associated with a spirit of adventure and the joy of discovery, representing the willingness to embark on new journeys and to learn from them.

Reversed Implications: When reversed, The Page of Wands can indicate a need for focus and direction, suggesting a refinement of potential and the development of a clearer purpose.

The Page of Wands in Personal Development: In the context of personal development, The Page of Wands symbolizes the journey of nurturing one's creative spirit and the importance of embracing the opportunities for growth and exploration.

"The Page of Wands" serves as a reminder of the vibrancy and potential that come with the early stages of any creative or intellectual endeavor. It encourages a youthful and enthusiastic approach to life's adventures, highlighting the value of curiosity, openness, and the joy of embarking on new and exciting paths.

Knight of Wands

"The Knight of Wands," a card in the Minor Arcana of tarot decks, symbolizes boldness, adventure, and a dynamic approach to life's challenges. This card typically depicts a figure, the Knight, who is characterized by energy, enthusiasm, and the spirit of adventure, often shown mounted on a spirited horse, symbolizing swift movement and a fearless pursuit of goals.

Psychologically, The Knight of Wands represents the aspect of personality that is driven by passion, ambition, and a desire for exploration. It signifies a time of action, where one is motivated by their aspirations and ready to take risks to achieve their goals. In readings, this card suggests a period of dynamic energy and enthusiasm, encouraging the querent to pursue their ambitions with boldness and confidence. It highlights the importance of channeling one's energies constructively and the exhilaration of embarking on new adventures. The Knight of Wands resonates with the Jungian archetype of the hero on a quest, embodying the qualities of charisma, daring, and the pursuit of a vision.

The presence of The Knight of Wands in a spread indicates a phase of vigorous activity and fearless exploration. It urges the querent to embrace their inner fire, to act on their passions, and to approach life's challenges with a bold and adventurous spirit.

When reversed, The Knight of Wands may suggest impulsiveness, recklessness, or unrefined ambition. It might indicate the need to temper one's enthusiasm with practicality or to reconsider the direction of one's energy and efforts.

"The Knight of Wands" thus symbolizes the journey of embracing one's ambitions and passions with courage and dynamism. It personifies the spirit of adventure and the readiness to face challenges head-on, emphasizing the importance of passion, energy, and the will to pursue one's dreams. The card encourages a bold approach to life, advocating for the value of enthusiasm, confidence, and the daring pursuit of one's goals.

Boldness and Adventure: The Knight of Wands underscores the themes of boldness and adventure, highlighting the dynamic energy and enthusiasm in pursuing one's ambitions.

Passion-Driven Action: The card emphasizes the importance of passion-driven action, inviting the querent to channel their energies constructively and to embrace the spirit of adventure.

Charisma and Daring: The Knight of Wands is often associated with charisma and the willingness to take risks, representing the fearless pursuit of goals and the exhilaration of new ventures.

Balancing Enthusiasm: When reversed, The Knight of Wands can indicate a need to balance enthusiasm with practicality, suggesting caution against impulsiveness or unrefined ambition.

The Knight of Wands in Personal Development: In the context of personal development, The Knight of Wands symbolizes the journey of harnessing one's passion and energy, fostering a courageous and adventurous approach to life's challenges and opportunities.

"The Knight of Wands" serves as a reminder of the power of ambition and the vitality of a spirited approach to life. It encourages embracing the journey with confidence and vigor, recognizing the value of passion, daring, and the bold pursuit of one's aspirations.

Queen of Wands

"The Queen of Wands," a card in the Minor Arcana of tarot decks, symbolizes confidence, charisma, and vibrancy. This card typically depicts a figure, the Queen, who is characterized by her strong, vibrant personality and her natural leadership qualities. She often appears seated on a throne, holding a wand, and is sometimes accompanied by a lion or other symbols of strength and courage, conveying her commanding presence and the warmth of her character.

Psychologically, The Queen of Wands represents the aspect of personality that is self-assured, creative, and nurturing, yet authoritative. It signifies a person who is able to inspire others with their enthusiasm and positivity. In readings, this card suggests a period where the querent might be embodying or encountering such qualities, encouraging them to embrace their confidence and to express their charisma and creativity. It highlights the importance of being assertive while maintaining warmth and approachability. The Queen of Wands resonates with the Jungian archetype of the mother figure or the nurturing leader, embodying qualities of empowerment, creativity, and the ability to motivate and care for others.

The presence of The Queen of Wands in a spread indicates a time of personal empowerment and positive influence. It urges the querent to step into their power, to harness their creative energies, and to lead with confidence and warmth.

When reversed, The Queen of Wands may suggest a lack of confidence, a struggle with self-expression, or an overbearing nature. It might indicate the need to balance one's assertiveness with empathy, or to reignite one's passion and creativity.

"The Queen of Wands" thus symbolizes the blend of confidence, creativity, and warmth. It personifies the charismatic and nurturing yet authoritative figure, emphasizing the importance of empowerment, positive influence, and the nurturing of one's creative impulses. The card encourages embracing leadership qualities, advocating for the value of inspiration, charisma, and the bold yet caring approach to life's challenges and opportunities.

Confidence and Charisma: The Queen of Wands underscores the themes of confidence and charisma, highlighting the vibrant energy and strong personality that characterize this figure.

Creativity and Empowerment: The card emphasizes the importance of creativity and empowerment, inviting the querent to express themselves boldly and to inspire others with their positivity.

Nurturing Leadership: The Queen of Wands is often associated with nurturing leadership, representing the ability to motivate and care for others while maintaining authority and strength.

Balanced Assertiveness: When reversed, The Queen of Wands can indicate a need to balance assertiveness with empathy, suggesting the importance of warmth and approachability in leadership.

The Queen of Wands in Personal Development: In the context of personal development, The Queen of Wands symbolizes the journey of embracing one's confidence, creativity, and leadership qualities, fostering a charismatic and nurturing approach to life's endeavors.

"The Queen of Wands" serves as a reminder of the power of a confident and creative spirit. It encourages embracing one's vibrancy and leadership potential, recognizing the value of charisma, creativity, and a nurturing yet authoritative approach in inspiring oneself and others.

King of Wands

"The King of Wands," a card in the Minor Arcana of tarot decks, represents charismatic leadership, vision, and an entrepreneurial spirit. This card typically features a figure, the King, who exudes confidence, authority, and the boldness to take initiative. He is often portrayed seated on a throne, holding a wand, symbolizing his command over his passions and his ability to lead and inspire others.

Psychologically, The King of Wands embodies the qualities of a dynamic leader who is driven by ambition and creativity. He signifies the capability to not only envision a bold future but also to take decisive action to make it a reality. In readings, this card suggests a period where the querent might be stepping into a leadership role or encountering someone who embodies these qualities. It encourages embracing one's own power to lead and to influence, highlighting the importance of ambition, innovation, and the ability to motivate others. The King of Wands resonates with the Jungian archetype of the ruler, combining the qualities of authority, creativity, and inspirational leadership.

The presence of The King of Wands in a spread indicates a time of decisive action and bold leadership. It urges the querent to take charge of their situation, to harness their creative energies, and to lead with confidence and charisma.

When reversed, The King of Wands may suggest arrogance, a lack of direction, or overbearing tendencies. It might indicate the need to temper one's assertiveness with humility, to reevaluate one's leadership approach, or to reignite one's visionary spark.

"The King of Wands" thus symbolizes the power of charismatic and visionary leadership. It personifies the qualities of confidence, creativity, and the ability to inspire and lead others, emphasizing the importance of taking initiative and the value of a bold, ambitious approach. The card encourages stepping into one's power, advocating for the significance of leadership, innovation, and the dynamic pursuit of one's goals.

Charismatic Leadership and Vision: The King of Wands underscores the themes of charismatic leadership and vision, highlighting the ability to inspire and lead with confidence and creativity.

Entrepreneurial Spirit and Decisive Action: The card emphasizes the importance of an entrepreneurial spirit and the readiness to take decisive action, inviting the querent to embrace their ambition and to make bold moves.

Inspirational Influence: The King of Wands is often associated with the capacity to influence and motivate others, representing the inspirational aspect of leadership and the impact of a commanding presence.

Balancing Leadership Qualities: When reversed, The King of Wands can indicate a need to balance leadership qualities, suggesting caution against arrogance or overbearing behavior.

The King of Wands in Personal Development: In the context of personal development, The King of Wands symbolizes the journey of embracing leadership potential, fostering qualities of ambition, innovation, and the ability to lead and inspire others.

"The King of Wands" serves as a reminder of the impact of visionary leadership and the importance of charisma, creativity, and ambition in guiding oneself and others towards success and fulfillment. It encourages a proactive and inspiring approach to life's challenges and opportunities, highlighting the value of assertiveness, vision, and the power of a dynamic, entrepreneurial spirit.

Conclusion:

As we reach the end of this journey through the mystical and insightful world of tarot, it's important to reflect on the rich tapestry of symbolism, intuition, and wisdom that these cards offer. Each card in the tarot deck is a mirror, reflecting aspects of our lives, our deepest desires, fears, challenges, and opportunities for growth. The practice of tarot reading is not just a method of divination; it's a path to self-discovery, offering a unique blend of psychological insight and spiritual guidance.

Tarot acts as a bridge between the conscious and the subconscious mind, revealing hidden truths and offering new perspectives. Each reading is a dialogue with oneself, a deep dive into the psyche, where the symbols and archetypes of the tarot interact with our personal experiences and beliefs. This interaction opens doors to understanding our inner world, helping us to navigate the complexities of life with greater clarity and purpose.

The beauty of tarot lies in its versatility and adaptability. It can be a tool for meditation, a guide for decision-making, a source of creativity, or a path for spiritual contemplation. Whether you're seeking answers to specific questions or exploring the depths of your soul, tarot provides a framework for introspection and self-exploration. It encourages us to pause, reflect, and consider different aspects of our lives from new angles.

As you continue your journey with tarot, remember that the true power of these cards lies within you. Your intuition, experiences, and the connections you make with the cards are what bring their messages to life. The tarot is a companion on your path, offering insights and reflections, but the wisdom to understand and apply these insights comes from your own inner guidance.

In the world of tarot, there is always more to learn and discover. Each card is a world of its own, rich with symbols, stories, and meanings that can evolve over time. Your relationship with the tarot will likely change and deepen as you continue to work with the cards, gaining new insights and developing your intuitive skills. The learning process is endless, and each reading can offer new revelations, no matter how familiar you are with the deck.

The community of tarot readers is a vibrant and diverse one, full of individuals from all walks of life who share a love for the cards and their wisdom. Engaging with this community, whether online or in person, can enhance your tarot journey, providing support, inspiration, and a wealth of shared knowledge. Remember, each reader brings their own unique perspective to the tarot, and there is much to be gained from sharing experiences and insights with others.

The practice of tarot is a personal and subjective one, shaped by your own beliefs, experiences, and intentions. There is no right or wrong way to read the cards; what matters most is your connection to them and the insights they bring. Trust in your intuition, be open to the messages of the cards, and allow yourself to be guided by the wisdom they offer.

As you continue to explore the depths of the tarot, you may find that the cards not only reveal insights about your life but also serve as catalysts for personal growth and transformation. They can challenge you to confront your fears, embrace your shadows, celebrate your strengths, and open your heart to new possibilities. The journey with the tarot is a transformative one, full of surprises, learning, and self-discovery.

In conclusion, the tarot is a powerful tool for exploration and insight, a mirror reflecting the multifaceted nature of our lives and our inner selves. It invites us to look deeper, to question, to reflect, and to grow. May your journey with the tarot be enriching, enlightening, and full of wonder. Embrace the journey, cherish the insights, and let the cards guide you on your path to greater understanding and self-discovery.

Resources

Books

" Degrees of Wisdom" by Rachel Pollack - This iconic book is often considered the bible of tarot reading. It delves deep into the symbolism and psychology of tarot, offering insightful interpretations and a rich understanding of the cards.

"The Ultimate Guide to Tarot Card Meanings" by Brigit Esselmont - This comprehensive guide covers detailed meanings for each tarot card, including various aspects of life like love, career, and spirituality, making it a go-to resource for both beginners and seasoned readers.

"The Tarot Bible" by Sarah Bartlett - An ideal book for beginners, offering an easy-to-understand overview of tarot. It covers everything from card meanings to how to conduct readings and spreads.

"Modern Tarot" by Michelle Tea - This book brings a fresh, contemporary perspective to tarot. It's perfect for those looking to connect the cards with everyday life, offering practical advice and personal anecdotes.

"Tarot for Your Self: A Workbook for Personal Transformation" by Mary K. Greer - A unique workbook that focuses on using tarot for personal development and self-exploration, filled with exercises and activities.

Websites

Biddy Tarot (biddytarot.com) - A treasure trove of tarot resources, offering free card meanings, guides, and blog posts. Their community and professional reader network offer opportunities for learning and sharing.

Labyrinthos (labyrinthos.co) - Known for its interactive and engaging approach to learning tarot, this site also offers a variety of free mobile apps to practice tarot readings.

Tarot.com - A comprehensive site for not only tarot readings but also astrology and numerology. It's a great resource for daily insights and deeper understanding of the cards.

Aeclectic Tarot (aeclectic.net) - Renowned for its extensive collection of tarot deck reviews. It's a great place to explore different decks and find one that resonates with you.

The Tarot School (tarotschool.com) - Offers a range of learning materials, including free tarot tips, audio lessons, and an in-depth tarot correspondence course.

Courses

Biddy Tarot Certification Program - Known for its structured approach and comprehensive content, this program offers certification, making it ideal for those looking to become professional tarot readers.

The Tarot School Correspondence Course - Perfect for those who prefer a self-paced, thorough study of tarot. It covers a wide range of topics in depth.

Tarot Professionals (tarotassociation.net) - This site offers a variety of courses and is known for its focus on the professional aspects of tarot reading, including ethics and business practices.

Udemy Tarot Courses - With a range of courses from various instructors, Udemy offers flexibility and a breadth of perspectives on tarot reading.

Mystery School Tarot (tarotinstitute.com) - This course is perfect for those interested in the spiritual and mystical aspects of tarot, offering a comprehensive approach to understanding the deeper layers of the cards.

Communities and Forums

The Tarot Forum (tarotforum.net) - A vibrant online community where enthusiasts and professionals alike discuss everything related to tarot, from deck reviews to interpretation help.

Reddit Tarot Community (r/tarot) - This subreddit is a lively place for tarot discussions, deck showcases, and sharing reading experiences.

Meetup (meetup.com) - A great resource to find local tarot meetups or groups. It's perfect for those looking to connect with other tarot enthusiasts in person.

Aeclectic Tarot Forums - Offers a welcoming space for tarot discussions, deck recommendations, and interpretations.

Facebook Groups - There are many tarot-focused groups where members share their experiences, seek advice, and discuss various tarot-related topics.

Podcasts and YouTube Channels

Tarot Bytes Podcast by The Tarot Lady - Offers bite-sized tarot lessons that are easy to digest, making it perfect for beginners.

Biddy Tarot Podcast - Brigit Esselmont hosts insightful discussions, and interviews with tarot professionals, and offers practical tips for tarot readings.

Kelly-Ann Maddox - Her YouTube channel is a rich resource for those interested in intuitive tarot reading, spiritual self-care, and personal growth.

Ethony - Offers a mix of tarot readings, deck reviews, and tutorials. Her channel is a great resource for diverse insights into tarot.

Remember, the practice of tarot is deeply personal and these resources are meant to offer a broad range of perspectives and techniques to enrich your understanding and practice.